Ben F. Williams, Jr.'s

MORE TALES
OF MY SOUTHWEST

Ben F Williams Jr.
DEC 2008

Ben F. Williams, Jr.'s

MORE TALES
OF MY SOUTHWEST

Smokin Z Press   Tucson, Arizona

To contact the author or order
additional copies of this book
write to us at:
P.O. Box 13121
Tucson, Arizona 85732
or visit the web site:
www.smokin-z.com

This edition was prepared for printing by
Ghost River Images
5350 East Fourth Street
Tucson, Arizona 85711
ghostriverimages.com

Edited by Eizabeth Ohm

Front and back cover photographs courtesy of
Glen "Gooch" Goodwin
P.O. Box 745
Patagonia, AZ 85624

Front cover images taken about five miles east of Lochiel, Arizona. Yucca stalk in the foreground is in the United States. The mountains and hills (Los Chivatos) are in Mexico.
Back cover image taken in the north end of the San Raphael Valley, looking at Saddle Mountain in the background.

ISBN: 978-0-9794800-1-0

Library of Congress Control Number: 2008909367

Printed in the United States of America

First Printing: November, 2008
10 9 8 7 6 5 4 3 2 1

Contents

Introduction

This is the second book of stories telling of my family's and my experiences while living on the United States-Mexico border. All of these tales are true of my own knowledge (or, as the lawyers might say, on information and knowledge upon which to form a belief and therefore I believe them to be true!). They are my very best recollection of the events upon which they are based. Some are reported from stories told to me by people in whom I have a great deal of faith as to their veracity.

It is my observation that the more I write, the more I want to write. Almost every story will bring to mind some other event which demands to be put on paper.

I hope my readers will find enough humor in these stories to activate their "tickle bones." When we are relegated to lives without some measure of humor, our existence becomes very dull and boring.

So, read and enjoy my tales!

Dedicated to my four great kids:
Liz, Diane, Katie, and Ben III

I'm proud to be your dad.

Acknowledgments

Thanks are due to friends, family, and colleagues who have inspired or assisted me in making this collection of stories possible: my lifelong love, Daisy; our children, to whom this book is dedicated; Glen "Gooch" Goodwin for his fabulous photographic art which graces this book's covers; Elizabeth Ohm, my most capable editor; Marilyn Bender, for constantly urging me and shaping and promoting ideas for more rewarding writing and book promotions.

There are a host of others to whom I am grateful, for their help or for their appearances as story characters, including Penny Porter, Don Dedera, Bill Kimble, Shelley Richey; Dr. Robert Montgomery; Sam Turner and fellow Quail Run writers; and many others whose names don't appear through unintentional oversight.

I thank you all.

HOME ON THE RANGE

BROWNIE'S DOWN

When Tooter and I were young boys, ages eight and nine, we often stayed with Granddad and Nana at the San Bernardino Ranch. One Saturday morning, we were out chasing rabbits with our BB guns down toward the Mexican border fence, about two hundred yards south of the barn.

On our way back to the ranch house, we passed through the corral and saw Brownie, Granddad's favorite saddle horse, lying on the ground on his side, with his legs extended. We walked up to Brownie. He looked at us with large, soulful eyes, which said, "Boys, I'm really sick and can't get up."

We talked to Brownie and tried to coax him onto his feet, without success. Not being able to help the poor suffering horse, we proceeded to the house, where Granddad was sitting on the porch smoking his morning cigar.

"Granddad, Brownie's down. He's layin' on his side in the corral at the barn and can't get up."

"I know, boys. Brownie's been in the mesquite beans and he's going to die."

"Granddad, isn't there something you can do to help Brownie?"

"Nope. I'm sorry, boys. He just ate too many of those mesquite beans, and there's not a thing in this world I can do for him. The closest vet is eighteen miles away in Douglas, and I don't have any way to load Brownie up to take him there.

I don't even know if a vet could help him. All we can do is just let nature take its course."

When mesquite beans ripen, they fall to the ground. If they get wet, the pods become rigid, much like the string that is used to tie hay bales.

When horses eat too many of the pods, they become impacted just as if they had been eating string made from hemp. This can cause the animal to die. Some people believe that the mesquite beans poison the animal. Not so. It's the impaction caused by the fibrous mesquite pods that's the villain.

In any event, poor old Brownie died, and Granddad and a couple of his cowboys hauled him out of the corral to a place where he was buried. At times nature seems cruel, and indeed it is.

[Note: Connie Kazal, who raises fine thoroughbred miniature horses, explained that mesquite beans are not poisonous and that it is the string-like pods that cause the problem.]

YOUNG AMERICAN COWBOYS

On the third Wednesday evening of July in 1941, I received a telephone call from my cousin Tooter.

"Benny, Dad and I are going to the ranch next Saturday morning and wondered if you would like to go."

I was thrilled with the invitation.

"Just a minute. Let me check with Mom and Dad."

On returning to the phone, "Tooter, they say it's fine and I can go. When and where should we meet?"

"Why don't you come by the house Friday evening, spend the night and then we'll be ready to go early Saturday morning."

Tooter had told me what a beautiful place it was. At one time it belonged to the Gabilondos, an old and well-known cattle-ranching family in Sonora. It was called "Rancho Nuevo" and boasted a stream of clear running water with blue channel catfish and native boney-tail trout.

We already knew from Dell, Tooter's father, how difficult the wily native boney-tails were to catch–much more so than the blue channels, a wary fish in their own right.

Although the end of July is at the height of the rainy season, it made little difference to us. Being just kids (Tooter was ten and I was twelve), we cared little about rain.

Concha, Tooter's pretty little paint pony, was a peach of a horse, well disciplined and gentle–just the ticket for a couple of young cowboys.

"Benny, there's a good brown horse for you at the ranch. I think you'll like him. Name's Pato."

Early in the morning before leaving, Aunt Louise, Tooter's mother, cooked a good, big breakfast for us. After a fine meal, we took off.

The road to Rancho Nuevo was by way of Geronimo Trail, a dirt, one-way lane proceeding east of Douglas over the Peloncillo Mountains, which divided Arizona and New Mexico, then on to Cloverdale, New Mexico. From there, we dropped south through the Henry Eicks ranch and crossed the border to Stewart Hunt's place in Mexico.

Once in Mexico, the road paralleled a clear stream of water that flowed through massive and beautiful sycamore trees. The sycamores were loaded with wild pigeons, which Dell told us were

Tooter and author, taken in 10th Street Park (now Raúl H. Castro Park) before leaving for Dell Williams' Mexico ranch, Rancho Nuevo

hunted as game birds, and good to eat. As the stream rambled through the canyon and sycamores, it occasionally pooled, and we could see fish in the clear water.

Dell told us that some *gringos* occasionally went to the Hunt ranch and camped next to the stream. They dynamited the pools to harvest the fish. Of course, the explosions killed everything, large and small. That didn't seem sportsmanlike to us.

When we finally arrived at Rancho Nuevo, I was surprised to see three mud buildings, the adobes of which had partially melted from the pelting of many years of rain. This was ranch headquarters. The buildings were roofed with rusted corrugated iron. Tooter and I were to learn that night when it rained what that rusty corrugated iron really meant. The whole place was not much to look at–a typical remote Mexican ranch, with rundown corrals and falling fence posts.

Dell employed a cowboy who lived on the place with his wife, Juanita. Juanita was the cook, and she was a good one. That evening for dinner Juanita charcoal grilled T-bone steaks and served them along with golden-brown french fries cooked to a crisp. These victuals, along with the customary *frijoles* and a dish of canned peaches for dessert, suited our palates completely.

It began to rain just as we were finishing dinner, and there being nothing to do, no electricity or radio, we went to bed. Dell showed us our bedroom and he took the other one.

Tooter and I retired to our room. No sooner had we gone to sleep than we were awakened by the dripping of water onto our faces from a leak in the roof. We got up and moved our beds to a dry spot, then went back to sleep. After a bit, the darn roof started leaking over the spot we had moved to. Well, we moved that blasted bed all over the bedroom six or eight times during the night, getting thoroughly soaked in the process, and cold to boot.

We peeked into Uncle Dell's room, where he was sleeping soundly under dry blankets. Not wanting to wake him by moving our bed into his room, we stayed put in our own quarters.

The next morning, we rose early, and Juanita cooked a good breakfast of bacon, eggs, toast, potatoes, hot coffee and *frijoles*. That breakfast really hit the spot.

Once finished with chow and shortly after it got light enough to get out and about, Dell had the cowboy bring our horses, already saddled, to the front yard. We mounted and rode off into a canyon of sycamores, scrub pines, manzanitas, and oaks.

"Benny, there are bear, lions, deer, turkeys and other wild game all over the place."

Shortly after Tooter spoke those words, two bucks jumped over the trail not thirty paces in front of us.

After riding for three hours, we returned to the ranch house. Dell had told us to bring our fishing tackle from Douglas. We got our fishing rods and proceeded to the creek. It was muddy from the previous night's rain. Crestfallen, thinking we wouldn't be able to catch fish in that muddy water, we soon discovered our mistake. With a shovel from the barn, we dug some angleworms from the soft earth near the creek. Using the juicy worms as bait, in no time at all fifteen boney-tails eight to ten inches long, and three blue-channel cats about a foot long, were in our creel.

Several wonderful hours were spent exploring the marvels and beauty of the place, the sounds of the water as it flowed through the rocks, the new smell of rain-dampened earth; orioles, blue jays, wild pigeons and yellow-colored finches looking just like mountain canaries as they darted from tree to tree; an occasional squirrel chasing another up a tree to their nest.

Later that evening, Juanita fried the fish in a cast-iron skillet greased with lard, after first dipping them in egg batter and rolling them in cornmeal, cooked so the outsides were crisp and the insides hot and steaming–they were delicious.

Dell, Tooter, and I all wolfed down a catfish and a couple of boney-tails. The boney-tails were well named for they were absolutely loaded with fine bones. The cats, on the other hand, were outstanding, as blue channels can be when properly prepared.

After dinner, Tooter and I went out into the yard, where Domingo, the *vaquero* (cowboy), was braiding a rawhide *riata*, a lariat used by cowboys for roping livestock. Many cowboys will tell you that after the *riata* has been braided, it should be properly greased with white kidney fat from a freshly-butchered beef.

Domingo showed me how to cut the rawhide into long strips for the braiding. He cut a slot approximately an inch-and-a-half deep and an inch-and-a-half wide in the top of a four-inch mesquite post. His pocket knife was razor-sharp. Domingo had already prepared the rawhide, which was in the form of a large circle. He had dampened it to make it pliable. Dry cowhide is hard as a rock and cannot be bent or cut without extreme difficulty.

Domingo placed the outer edge of the round circle of the hide against the protruding part of the post, and then pulled it toward himself against the knife's keen edge so that a quarter-inch strip was cut cleanly from the skin. Depending on how big the circle of hide was, one could make a strip from its edge one hundred feet or more in length. Some Mexican cowboys can handle a rawhide *riata* seventy-five feet long, and some are even longer.

That evening, Domingo showed Tooter and me how to make a quirt. A quirt is a short whip, eighteen to twenty-four inches long. First he took the strips of rawhide he had already cut, which were pliable because they were damp, and braided them around a bolt, which made the hard part of the quirt's handle. Then he braided the pliable part beyond the bolt down to the end. Leather strips were

Ben F. Williams, Jr.

GOBIERNO DEL ESTADO DE SONORA
DEPARTAMENTO DE GANADERIA

Número ___00010___

Habiéndose cumplido los requisitos que son al efecto necesarios, se expide al señor DELL WILLIAMS DEL RIO, con domicilio en Agua Prieta, Sonora,

EL TITULO DE LA MARCA DE HERRAR Y SEÑAL DE SANGRE

cuyos diseños aparecen a continuación, para acreditar en los términos de la Ley de Ganadería vigente y de las demás disposiciones relativas, la propiedad de sus semovientes.

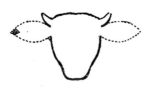 

DESCRIPCION DE LA SEÑAL DE SANGRE:

OREJA DERECHA.- HORQUETA EN EL EXTREMO.

OREJA IZQUIERDA: NADA.

Y para los usos legales correspondientes, se extiende el presente de acuerdo con el artículo 18 de la Ley antes citada, en Hermosillo, Sonora, a los veinte días del mes de marzo, - de mil novecientos cuarenta y cinco.

SUFRAGIO EFECTIVO.-NO REELECCION.

El Jefe del Depto. de Ganadería,
Hilario Olea Jr.

D. G.-2

GOBIERNO DEL ESTADO DE SONORA
DEPARTAMENTO DE GANADERIA
Número __00010__

REGISTRO de 1 señor DELL WILLIAMS DEL RIO, criador(es) de ganado bovino, con asiento de producción en el rancho de "Rancho Nuevo" Municipio de Agua Prieta, Sonora, inscrito bajo el número 10 a fojas número 1 del Libro respectivo, siendo su marca de herrar la que aparece al reverso.

Hermosillo, Son, a 20 de marzo de 1945

Dell Williams' Rancho Nuevo Flying X certified brand certificate inserted to fashion the end pieces of the quirt.

I was fascinated, and with Domingo's help cut some strips to make a small quirt which I took home to Douglas. This was my new key holder.

When night fell, Tooter and I retired to our bedroom–this time after the bedding had dried in the sun–and there being no more rain, we slept like the dead.

Early the next morning, Juanita served us another great breakfast–this time oatmeal, eggs, toast, and of course, *frijoles*. On most Mexican ranches, no meal is complete without a small plate of *frijoles*.

After breakfast, Dell said, "Well, boys, I've got to get back to town, so we'll be leaving in a few minutes. I hope you had a good time."

"We had a great time!"

I told Uncle Dell, "I learned how to fish in the murky waters and found that they bite better when the water's not clear. I also learned how to braid rawhide and leather. Thanks for a wonderful trip."

So back to town and school we went, two happy, but tired, young American cowboys.

THE WORRISOME RAT

Ezra J. "Bud" Warner and his wife, Dorothy "Dolly," bought the Cienega Ranch ten miles north of Rodeo, New Mexico, in 1937. Bud was heir to a large fortune which originated from Sprague-Warner Company, reputedly one of the largest wholesale grocery companies in the United States. Prior to buying the Cienega Ranch, Warner lived like a playboy off his inheritance.

The ranch headquarters is nestled prettily under stately giant cottonwood trees originally placed as corral fence posts around the house. The posts took root and proliferated into a beautiful, inviting, and shady cottonwood grove. The Cienega derived its name from an underground watercourse which runs in a low valley to the east of the house. It occasionally surfaces, creating ponds which are home to native yellow catfish. One afternoon, Dolly and I caught thirty-three of those catfish, each about nine inches long, which we took back to the ranch, where Lucas cooked them for dinner.

Bud had hired Lucas as cook, taking him away from Dad's Palomas Ranch in Chihuahua. After Lucas' arrival, the cuisine at the Cienega was always top-flight.

After his supper, it was Bud's custom to read in an easy chair in his living room. One evening he noticed a shadow dart across the floor to the corner of the room. A closer inspection revealed that it was a big rat. The rat disappeared. *Now where would that rat be hiding?* he wondered.

The following night he found rat droppings in another part of the room and noticed the scampering rodent once again. This time Bud saw the rat run into a hole in the corner of the baseboard of the room.

Bud drove to town the following morning and bought some rat traps. Setting them out for Mr. Rat, he carefully baited them with a most succulent cheese and peanut butter concoction from Lucas' kitchen larder.

Early the next morning, Bud found his traps empty, with the bait gone. He replaced the cheese and peanut butter, then reset the traps.

That evening, after supper and a few highballs, Bud settled down to read a book on the history of the South. While reading about General Sherman's march on Atlanta, a quick movement in the corner of the room caught his eye, and he again saw Mr. Rat scampering around his living room. Bud noticed that the rat returned to the corner of the room and again dove down into a small hole under the baseboard.

The following night was a repeat performance. The trap remained empty. Bud was becoming frustrated.

The next day, after so many unsuccessful tries, Bud thought, *I'm gonna get you tonight, Mr. Rat.* He positioned his easy chair so it was facing directly toward the corner where the rat's sally port was located. He took his .410 shotgun from the closet, loaded it, and carefully cradled the weapon in his lap, waiting for Mr. Rat's nightly appearance.

Sure enough, after a bit, the rat poked his nose up out of the hole. Bud was ready for him. He instantly aimed and fired, blowing a very large hole in the baseboard of the room. The rat disappeared.

No more Mr. Rat, just a big hole in the corner of the room.

CLOSE CALL

When I was fourteen years old, I spent the summer with my aunt and uncle, Ella and Morris Browder, at the San Bernardino Ranch seventeen miles east of Douglas. There were some fertile farms on the ranch. Morris, who had retired from the Southern Pacific Railroad, wanted to try his hand at farming. For many years he had a game leg, and it was causing him more and more trouble as he got older, and therefore he wanted a more relaxed form of life. (Question: Farming is an easier form of life?)

One day, Morris told me to take the Chevrolet ranch truck down to the farm and bring some shovels back to the house. I had just learned to drive and had never driven the big Chevy. It had a stick gearshift with a leaf-like mechanism just under the knob of the shift. You had to depress the clutch to change gears–all new to me. Nevertheless, I felt I could drive it.

I took my Winchester .22 pump rifle, which I always carried with me in the event I ran into a coyote, bobcat, or wolf. These animals can be very dangerous to newborn livestock and will kill and eat them.

The Winchester had a hammer action. I propped the rifle against the seat, with the butt on the floor and the barrel pointed up toward the roof of the cab. The rifle was loaded. The hammer was at half-cock, which meant that it was on "safety."

As I was driving to the farm, I hit a couple of rough spots in the road, causing the truck to jump. This caused me to bounce, along with the rifle, almost to the roof of the truck. The rifle jumped up from the floor, moving the hammer from half-cock to full-cock. When we came down with a hard knock, the rifle fired, missing my head by only a few inches. It left a beautiful hole in the roof of the cab.

It literally scared the daylights out of me. I had to stop the truck in order to regain my composure and think up what kind of story I could tell my uncle about the new hole in the roof of his truck.

I don't remember now what I told him, but I sure do remember the incident and the safety lesson learned: that when in a vehicle of any type, be sure your weapon is unloaded and the barrel pointed at the floor. Then, if the weapon for any reason fires, you will kill the motor and not yourself.

Talk about a near miss–that was as near as I'd ever like to get.

THE PALOMAS GYPSIES

During the 1940s at the Palomas headquarters (Nogales hacienda), a band of gypsies made their camp under some large cottonwood trees. They had stayed six weeks and there was no indication that they were disposed to move on. It seemed they had found a new home. As the old cowboy saying goes, "They had found a bird's nest on the ground."

The hacienda's policy of hospitality for travelers was too good to be true. Free grub in the ranch cowboy dining room, prepared by Lucas and the cooking staff. Camping facilities in the cottonwood grove. All without charge to travelers. No time limit on length of stay.

When gypsies are mentioned, one envisions women with black hair and dark eyes–sultry, sexy vixens adorned with gold bracelets halfway up their arms, looking like Hedy Lamarr in the 1940s Hollywood movies. Men with colorful bandanas and wearing vividly colored silk shirts, all riding in horse-drawn covered wagons.

Not so the Palomas gypsies. They arrived in their typical mule-drawn covered wagons but wore traditional garb like Mexican vaqueros, light-colored straw hats for the men and cotton cloth bandanas for the women. They were somewhat sullen, and they spoke a Chihuahuan Spanish dialect. For example, "saddle" in Chihuahua was called a *silla* (chair) while the Mexicans of Sonora called it a *montura*.

They were clannish and didn't mix well with the general ranch population.

Hard physical labor was shunned. A gypsy worked only when he had to in order to feed and clothe himself. Wanderers they were, nomads who moved about the country living off the land or people who might be disposed to help them.

As mentioned, the policy of the Nogales hacienda was to provide free meals and lodging or campsites for transients so they could rest from the rigors of their journey. Travel conditions in those days were rough–over bumpy dirt roads, mostly trails–and people were few and lived far from each other. With good food and a place to rest for as long as they wished, no wonder so many gypsies came.

The headquarters had a large dining room where single cowboys and transients could take their meals. Living quarters were available at the hacienda for married cowboys and their families, who ate in their own apartments. The gypsies and single men, however, ate in the cowboys' and travelers' dining room.

This hospitality became so well known throughout the region that more and more gypsies arrived with increasing frequency and stayed because of good food and accommodations. It finally became necessary to impose a rule that travelers were welcome to food and lodging, but for a period not to exceed one week.

Once the new rule was imposed, gypsy visits became less frequent. Visitors had to pull up stakes and continue traveling after a week's sojourn at the Palomas Ranch headquarters. This new policy terminated the "bird's nest on the ground."

And so far as I know, we never received the "gypsy curse."

THE SCABBARD

One evening at the Palomas, Vic said, "Benny, tomorrow I'd like to go down to Rafael Gabilondo's ranch for a visit. We bought some heifers from him not too long ago, and I want to make arrangements for their delivery. I'm pretty sure you'll enjoy meeting the old gentleman, and certainly you'll like his ranch."

The Gabilondo ranch was quite a distance south of the Coyote pasture, the southernmost pasture of the Palomas.

Early the next morning, off we went in Vic's Chevy coupe, arriving at Don Rafael's ranch late in the morning.

Don Rafael was a fine gentleman of advanced age, somewhere in his late eighties as best I could determine. On arrival, we found him on his front porch in a rocking chair, with a case of Carta Blanca beer in small bottles at his side. He was rockin' and drinkin' and obviously enjoying himself. When nature required, he would step out of his chair, walk over to the edge of the porch, and pee.

I didn't understand Spanish in those days, but Vic was completely bilingual, so he and the old man talked about heifers and events of the day.

After a short spell, Don Rafael asked Vic to inquire of me if I had a good pocket knife.

"I sure do. It's an 'old-timer' make, and I've put a razor's edge on it." I was proud of that knife.

"Let me borrow it," said Don Rafael. He called one of his cowboys and told him to make a belt scabbard for it.

In about an hour, the knife was returned in the finest leather scabbard you ever saw. I carried it on my belt for many years.

We enjoyed a delicious lunch with Don Rafael before returning to the Palomas late in the afternoon.

A most enjoyable day, and indeed an interesting old gentleman.

FRESH MEAT

We had been out of meat for ten days at the Las Palmas Ranch in Chihuahua, Mexico. Pilo, the cook, told me the men really missed meat, so I told him I would go get a deer if he would fix it for us. He said, "*Pues si, como no,*" which means, "Yes, you bet."

My sidekick, Benjamín Sandoval, and I took off at dawn the next morning in the Jeep. We drove to the foot of the Dog Mountains north of the ranch house. It was four miles and took us forty minutes, as there were no roads and our path led over rough terrain.

The ranch, if you will picture it in your mind's eye, was located around the southwestern tip of New Mexico as it juts into Mexico. Las Palmas ranch headquarters was four miles south of the U.S.-Mexico boundary line. The mountains where we went for the deer were just south of the border fence.

We parked the Jeep at the foot of the mountains and proceeded to climb on foot. I carried Dad's .300 Savage which we kept at the ranch. Almost every ranch in those days had one or more guns–necessary at times for predators or intruders. We always had a firearm with us when traveling around the country. Wolves and coyotes were death on newborn livestock, and a good rifle and marksman were just what the doctor ordered to fix the problem.

Benjamín's eyesight was phenomenal. He could see a flyspeck on the wall at twenty yards. We were about halfway up one of the steep hills when he said

"*Párate. Alli está un venado.*" (Stop. There's a deer.)

I looked up, and sure enough, about 250 yards away on a ridge stood a beautiful buck. I dropped to one knee, took aim, and fired. The buck fell over dead. Benjamín exclaimed, "*Buen tiro!*" (Good shot!)

"*Pues, seguro.*" (Well, sure!) My marksmanship was phenomenal that day.

I had always known that Benjamín was part Indian. Some Indian lore says that the first thing to do when you kill a deer is drink its warm blood; it will make you strong and virile. In Benjamín's case, it sure didn't work. In fact, it backfired.

When we got to the animal, Benjamín said, "Okay, we cut the deer's throat so that he will bleed and the flesh will not be tainted with blood."

"Okay," I responded.

"The next thing is to open the deer's chest." A lot of blood had accumulated by this time in the cavity.

"Next we scoop up a handful of blood and drink it while it's still warm. It'll make your heart strong, and it's good for you."

"*Ni modo, Benjamín.*" (No way, Benjamín, not on your life.) Since I had no Indian blood running through my veins, I felt no need to strengthen my heart, certainly not by Benjamín's method.

My *tocayo* (same name) cupped his hands, scooped out a large handful of blood and promptly drank it down. In about thirty seconds, he became violently ill and began retching all over the mountainside. He had to sit down, for he couldn't stand. He was really sick. I never saw a sicker man.

Well, I was in a real pickle because I couldn't carry either Benjamín or the deer off the mountain without help. We sat and waited for about half an hour until Benjamín was able to get up and walk.

"Are you able to climb down to the Jeep?" I asked.

"Yes, and I'll help you with the deer. I'm feeling better now."

The two of us carried the deer off the mountain.

When we got back to the ranch, Cookie promptly removed the deer's loin. He ground it up and from that made *albondigas* (meatball stew) with onions, potatoes, carrots, and tomatoes–a really delicious dish. If one didn't think about the hunt, the venison was by far more tasty.

Let me ask you: Do you think warm, fresh deer blood will make you stronger and more virile?

RANCH GRUB
or
COWBOY VITTLES

Vic kept a gallon jug of mescal in the closet of his bedroom at the ranch. In the jug with the mescal was a Maguey worm. He swore that his mescal was the finest, that the worm absorbed all its impurities.

Although I was only sixteen when I spent that summer at the Palomas with Victor Gabilondo, it was his custom, and he encouraged me (a willing participant), to have a short "snort" before dinner each evening–a straight shot of mescal, with a lick of salt and a bite of lemon.

I was delighted to participate in the appetizer because it gave me a robust appetite to better enjoy the fine repasts that Lucas, the ranch cook, always served. Also, I felt I had come of age, being able to partake of liquor as grown men did.

Lucas came from Casas Grandes, a town four hours away by truck. He had been in charge of the kitchen at the Nogales hacienda for several years. In addition to cooking and supervising meals for Vic and his guests, Lucas took care of feeding the single cowboys and transients as well.

Another of Lucas' duties was to oversee the distribution of food staples such as beans, flour, coffee, lard, baking powder, and sugar for the men working the fence camps. When the ranch was purchased in 1941 by the Williams group, fences had to be built, repaired, or replaced. There were over 1,000 miles of barbed wire fences on the place when it was bought. Six crews, six men to a crew, constantly repaired or built fences to meet ranch requirements. Of course, the workers needed food.

Regularly, a man and pack mule came in from each of the camps for grub. Lucas saw to it that their needs were filled from the food inventory. When necessary, a large truck went to Casas Grandes for foodstuff, purchased in bulk—beans and flour a ton at a time, and other provisions by the case. It was up to Lucas to keep enough food on hand to supply the hungry workers.

I frequently asked Vic to have Lucas bake a chocolate cake for us for dinner.

"Sure," came the reply, and after dinner would appear the most delicious morsel you ever put in your mouth, built from the ground up, without fancy mixes.

One time Dad took Bud Warner, a good friend, to the ranch. Bud tasted Lucas' wares, and I'll be darned if he didn't hire him to come to the United States to live and cook for him and his wife, Dorothy. The Warners owned the Cienega Ranch ten miles north of Rodeo, New Mexico. Lucas worked for Bud and Dolly, as she was known, for several years until they sold the place.

Ah, such sweet memories!

BAMBI

I spent the summer of 1946 at Dad's Las Palmas Ranch in Chihuahua. After breakfast one morning, I said to Tom Ferrel, the ranch superintendent, "Let's go over to the Nogales hacienda and see Vic and Mary Gabilondo. It's been a long time since I've seen them, and we could visit, have a good lunch, and maybe a piece of Lucas' chocolate cake."

"That's a great idea, Benny. I have to talk to Vic anyway about some strays that have gotten through the fence on us, and I want to know where to put them back."

Lucas, their cook, made the best chocolate cake I ever ate. It could attract people like molasses draws flies. Tom and I hadn't had a good dessert for a long time.

We proceeded to the Nogales hacienda, where Mary and Vic graciously greeted us. They always knew when visitors approached because a small flock of peacocks and guinea hens which roosted on the windmill tower out in the side yard announced strangers approaching from miles away. They made the loudest screeching sounds a body ever heard.

We had a nice visit and the cake was even better than I remembered. During lunch, Mary asked, "By the way, Benny, have you met Bambi?"

"Who is Bambi?"

"She's my pet deer."

"Where did you get a pet deer?"

"One day the cowboys brought me a young fawn, just a baby. They found her in the mountains abandoned by her mother. I made a nipple from a rubber glove by poking a small hole in the end of a finger, then filling it with warm milk and a little touch of molasses. I fed that

Palomas Ranch headquarters (Nogales), in front of Bambi's mountain

fawn for a long time until it reached full growth. I named her Bambi.

"Whenever I went out in the back yard and called Bambi, she would come down out of the mountain to get a cube of sugar and a hug. She became a great pet, and I derived a lot of pleasure from our association. When she got old enough to fend for herself, I knew I had to set her free in the Sierra Madre Mountains behind the ranch house. But before I did that, I tied a red ribbon around her neck so that hunters would see the ribbon and not shoot her. I'll go call her right now and see if she'll come to me."

Sure enough, a young doe pranced down the mountain wearing a red ribbon around her neck. The obvious bond of affection between the two was clearly apparent. The deer leaned against Mary while she scratched behind her ears. She nuzzled her hand in search of the well-remembered warm milk sweetened with molasses when she was a young fawn. Mary sometimes had a special surprise, a piece of apple or a fresh carrot stick.

After our good lunch (with cake), Tom and I returned to Las Palmas. Several months later I saw Mary again and asked her about Bambi.

"I went out in the back yard one day and called for Bambi, but she never came. I don't know what happened to her. Probably a lion or hunter got her, but I never saw her again."

Sometimes it's a mistake to interfere with Mother Nature and make a pet of a wild animal.

BILL ADAMS

Bill Adams was a cattleman who owned a ranch south of the Palomas ranch in Chihuahua, Mexico. He called his place the Beresford. Adams owned one of the finest herds of Black Angus cattle to be found anywhere in the Republic of Mexico. He had about 1,500 head.

Bill was a pilot who owned an airplane, which he kept hangared at the Beresford. Occasionally he would fly his plane to the Nogales ranch headquarters, buzz the house a couple of times, and then land in the pasture to the north of the house. We knew when he buzzed the hacienda that he wanted us to come and pick him up. We drove a pickup out to the plane to get him.

On one occasion, Bill flew up to visit with Vic Gabilondo, the ranch superintendent, and me. During lunch, Bill told us about a fine registered Angus bull he had bought for his herd. He said he had paid several thousand dollars for the sire, and he was a beauty to behold.

"Benny, would you like to fly down with me to my place and see the bull? Vic, why don't you come along, too?"

Vic was busy that afternoon and couldn't go, so that left me as Bill's only passenger. I was delighted to fly with him. It was only about twenty minutes by air but several hours by automobile.

Bill was always involved in some interesting project and eager to talk about it. His new Angus stud and his plans to improve the Beresford herd were paramount subjects on that day. Bill couldn't wait to fly me to his ranch and show off "Ferd," his new pride and joy.

At the Beresford, Bill took me to a special pen to see Ferd. He was indeed a fine looking animal; Bill was entitled to be proud of such a specimen.

When Bill was a young cowpuncher in his early twenties, he had gone to work as *caporál* or straw boss for my grandfather, Marion Williams, at his Santa Rosa ranch west of Nacozari, Sonora. My father was then a young man, living and working on the ranch. Dad and Bill had a misunderstanding which fostered a fistfight in which Dad had prevailed. Bill went to Granddad and told him of the fight.

"This ranch isn't big enough for him and me. One of us has to go."

"Well, you know who that will be, Bill."

So Bill left, and it was a number of years before Dad saw him again. Over the years, they did rekindle their friendship.

Bill became manager of Col. Bill Greene's famous 4C Cananea Cattle Company ranch. He was still flying his airplane. I recall his coming into our office at the Gadsden Hotel and telling us how somebody had been involved at the Cananea ranch fostering labor problems. Cananea was and still is a mining town with a strong union or *sindicato* presence. At times there have been deadly riots. People have been killed in anti-gringo demonstrations in and around the community. They had poured sugar into Bill's aircraft gas tank and almost caused a fatal accident.

In later years, Bill retired to El Paso, where he ultimately died. Dad was an honorary pallbearer at his funeral. Bill Adams was a true spirit of the west–a real cowboy.

BEFORE MY TIME

JESÚS GARCIA

On the red enameled mantel above the fireplace in the guest house of what at one time was the back bedroom rested a twisted piece of iron rail two feet long, with jagged edges at each end. This was the product of a tremendous explosion which happened on November 7, 1907, in Nacozari, Sonora, seventy miles south of Douglas.

When I first saw the jagged piece of steel, I was with my father during a trip to his mine near Nacozari. Dad's mining company, Compania Minera Benwilco, was in full swing, operating a copper and molybdenum mine southeast of Nacozari. The company's offices were in Nacozari, where Benwilco had leased the old Moctezuma Copper Company guest house on the hill above the town. The house was known locally as Casa Blanca (the white house).

On the afternoon of November 7, 1907, a narrow-gauge company train loaded with 160 boxes filled with four tons of dynamite had caught fire after leaving Nacozari on its way to the Pilares (pillars) mine. Thinking quickly, Jesús Garcia, the engineer, drove the locomotive to a higher elevation. He kept it from rolling back into the town by putting the wheels in reverse and putting sand on the rails. In this way he was able to keep the "bomb" from exploding in the town of Nacozari, losing his life in the process.

The explosion occurred at 2:20 p.m., killing several people, but through Jesús Garcia's heroic efforts, the town, with a population of approximately 6,000 people, was saved. Had the train rolled back down the hill into town, the powder magazine, containing 100,000 pounds of dynamite, would have exploded, along with two enormous gas-filled tanks, and many more people would have died.

The heroic act was heralded worldwide and monuments to Jesús Garcia were erected in many places in Mexico and South America.

At the time, Rawhide Jimmy Douglas and his family were residing in Nacozari. Rawhide's young four-year-old son recalled the explosion. That boy was to become a good friend of my father, and eventually they became associated in a mining venture together in Mexico.

The story is told of Jesús' mother, the young widow Rosa Corona, viuda de Garcia, and her eight children who had traveled from Hermosillo, Sonora, in 1898 to settle in Nacozari. Nacozari was a booming copper mining town with a population of around 5,000. Miners' pay was one dollar (two pesos) per day, which was five to ten times more than the national average for wages paid in the rest of the Republic.

Nacozari as it looked in Jesús Garcia's time. *Photo courtesy of Phelps Dodge Collection.*

Nacozari acquired the pet name of *El Real* (Spanish silver coin of value) because of its prosperity and the fact that business could be transacted on a cash basis by payment in silver coins.

A new railroad line was built so that Phelps Dodge's mines at Nacozari could ship their copper concentrates to Douglas for smelting. Prior to building the rail line, goods were brought into Nacozari in large eight-foot tall wagons drawn by eighteen-to-twenty-mule teams.

After introduction of rail service, the town prospered, boasting secondhand stores, pharmacies, barber shops, bakeries, a general store, fruit stands, and saloons, many in number. Businesses were given such names as a secondhand store called *Nomeolvidas al Pasar* (don't forget me in passing), a pawn shop named *Monte de Ciadad* (the mountain of pity), a general store called *El Precio Fijo* (the fixed price) and a fruit stand called *La Cascara de Oro* (the golden husk). There were many saloons with Mexican names translated as the dove, the black cat, the little rooster, I am laughing, and such is life.

Rosa Corona's husband, Francisco García-Pino, had been a blacksmith in Hermosillo and also at a small mining community to the east called Batuc.

While en route from Hermosillo with his wife and eight children, Francisco died. As closely as can be determined, he had a ruptured appendix. His son, Jesús, had been an apprentice in his father's blacksmith shop. There he learned the basics of mechanics. This knowledge, along with an innate grasp of machinery, made it possible for him to become an apprentice railway engineer. It was said that Jesús García was courageous, studious, quick-witted, friendly, and popular. He was well liked by his friends and colleagues and nicknamed *El Guero* (the blond one).

The widow Rosa García maintained her brood of eight by operating a small restaurant where her savory food included sweet rolls, cinnamon-flavored pastries, and hominy with meat, as well as vegetable and meat soups. On feast days, the café would feature venison roast, turkey, or tamales and Sonoran-style enchiladas stacked like pancakes.

When Jesús reached seventeen years of age, he decided to venture out on his own and directly approached the mining company's railroad boss, W.L. York, asking for a job. After starting as a water boy, he then cleaned locomotives. As he grew older and stronger, he was given a job on the section gang which maintained railroad track. Later he became a brakeman, then a fireman and, at age twenty, a locomotive engineer. With the more advanced jobs came raises in pay so that Jesús was able to help his mother and family move to a better home with running water and electric lights.

With his new and more responsible jobs, Jesús became a confident young man-about-town. He frequently dressed in suits with tie and wore a cowboy hat tilted on the back of his head. He sometimes wore a moustache. Jesús became an expert horseman, as did most young Mexican men. By the time he had reached the age of twenty-four, he was engaged to Maria de Jesús Soqui, an eligible young maiden. On the night of November 6, 1906, Jesús, the young romantic, hired a band of mariachis and all went together to Maria's home where they serenaded her much of the night.

When Jesús reported for work on the morning of November 7, 1907, he was told that Albert Biel, the conductor, was in the hospital. The conductor would normally oversee switching and loading operations and issue orders as to when and where the train moved and stopped. Without a conductor, everybody on the crew must work harder, which included Jesús, who was put in charge because of Biel's absence. Jesús drove Locomotive number 2, which he had so carefully cleaned, decorated, and cared for over a long period of time.

The Pilares mine is six miles distant from the center of Nacozari, at an elevation of 2,000 feet above the townsite. Jesús García's crew for the day was José Romero, his fireman, and a brakeman. García's job was to move all empty ore cars up the incline to large ore bins and dump the ore into the rail cars. García had to move twenty empty cars to the mine site, disconnect them and then at a switching area called *El Porvenir*, see that his locomotive was attached to twenty full ore cars to take back down the mountain. When the ore train reached the bottom, he moved them onto a trestle which overhung the ore crushers. The cars, designed to swivel and tilt, unloaded the ore into the crushers. This procedure was accomplished by the brakeman, and once the cars were empty, the train went back up the incline to the mine for more ore.

On the morning of November 7, after Jesús second round trip to the mine, a company messenger swung aboard his train and relayed an order informing García that more supplies were needed at the mine.

"Take the train to the lower yard and talk with Mr. Elizondo. You will only need five cars. He will tell you what the freight is."

Once at the lower level, Elizondo informed Jesús that four tons of dynamite were to be transferred from the powder magazine to two of Garcia's ore cars. Other materials and supplies would be loaded into the other three cars to be taken to the mine.

The dynamite used in the mining operation had been shipped from Oakland, California, by rail to Nacozari, where it was stored in a stone-and-mortar building close to the railroad in a powder magazine containing 2,000 boxes of dynamite. The magazine contained detonating caps and fuses as well.

While the five cars were being loaded, the crew went to lunch.

Nacozari had no automobiles or trolley, so the mining company's offices, workshop, and storehouses were within easy walking distance of each other. The town also had a gas plant and large storage tanks where gas was manufactured in Nacozari to be stored and used in the power plant to generate electricity for the town.

When Jesús returned to his train after lunch, he was irritated to see that the workers in the yard had allowed the fire in his boiler to almost go out. This may have distracted somebody from observing the rule that rail cars bearing explosives were always to be placed at the rear of the train.

Not so on that day. Loaded in the first two cars behind the locomotive were four tons of dynamite. The two cars bearing dynamite were attached immediately behind the engine, a breach of company rules that would never have been allowed had the train's conductor been on duty.

Another breach of company rules was that a faulty smokestack had not been corrected to prevent live sparks from being pushed out of the stack.

With the fire newly rebuilt in the firebox, but not yet enough steam to make a full boost of power, García opened the throttle as the train began to move ahead, gaining speed and causing sparks from the faulty smokestack to blow into the first two cars among the dynamite boxes. As the train was moving, an American passerby shouted, "Hey, look, there! Smoke in the powder!"

Yet another problem was the fact that the train's brakeman, Francisco Rendón, was not on duty. It was his day off.

With a strong breeze fanning the fire, the blaze intensified. Two trainmen had removed their jackets and were attempting to beat out the flames, but without success.

Dynamite by itself will normally burn without exploding. However, fuses and detonating caps subjected to fire will explode with sufficient strength to cause the dynamite to also explode.

Jesús was well aware of the fact that there were at least 100,000 pounds of dynamite stored in the magazine in Nacozari, as well as the two large tanks of combustible gas and other flammables in warehouses throughout the town.

Jesús saw that the efforts of the two trainman were futile, and he ordered them to jump and save themselves. He opened the throttle to full, attempting to propel the train ahead to a level point where he could also jump off and save himself.

Four Mexican miners were waiting for the train in order to catch a ride to Pilares. Just short of the flat grade where Jesús could turn the train loose and jump to safety, several observers saw him wildly waving his hat and shouting words that were not heard by residents along the way.

At 2:20 in the afternoon, there occurred a horrendous explosion which shook the entire community with a resounding noise that was heard several miles away. The cars containing the dynamite were blown into smithereens.

Jesús had been able to propel the locomotive to a point beyond a small rise separating his train from the main part of town. Jimmy Douglas' four-year-old son said later that he would never forget the noise (clap! boom!) of the explosion. Locomotive and train parts, as well as rail and pieces of metal, were thrown upon the town, tearing through roofs. A part of an old car was hurled through the air two-and-one-half miles from the point of explosion onto a mountainside.

Thomas C. Romney, a construction boss who was working near the center of town, later wrote an eyewitness account:

"I observed the train of cars winding its way . . . the train seemed to be on fire. I watched it with interest and with considerable curiosity until the last car had passed over the summit of the hill when almost immediately there occurred the most horrific explosion that I had ever witnessed. The force of the concussion was so violent that it seemed to me my head would be blown from my shoulders and as if by instinct I found my hands locked over the top of my head to keep it from being blown into space.

"After the shock was over, I went at top speed to the summit of the hill to discover what happened.

"The sight . . . haunts me still . . . a dead man lying on his back with the warm blood from his body flowing under the hill in a small rivulet . . . the warehouse . . . so completely demolished that not a particle of evidence remained . . . even the solid shelf of rock on which the building stood received a scar fully three feet deep. Off to the left . . . had stood a tenement house that had sheltered several families. Not one stick of timber was in its original position."

The four waiting miners were killed, along with a boy named Chisholm, who was struck by a bullet-like rivet. He had been standing 200 yards from the point of explosion.

The wooden section houses were destroyed and collapsed on the bodies of seven women and children. Eighteen other residents and workmen of the upper yard were injured as well.

It was the duty of the brothers and brothers-in-law of Jesús García to recover his body and take it home. They identified the body by his boots.

Through his completely courageous and unselfish act, Jesús García had saved the town of Nacozari and undoubtedly several hundred people from death.

James S. Douglas, my father's friend and general manager of the Moctezuma Mining Company, was in Cananea when he received the news at 4:00 p.m. on November 7 of the explosion in Nacozari. He dropped everything and traveled to Nacozari from Cananea by way of Douglas. Upon arriving in Nacozari and learning the facts, he telegraphed Sonoran governor Luis E. Torres in Hermosillo as follows:

"Esteemed General: Seventy boxes of dynamite caught on fire by flying sparks from the locomotive yesterday at 2 P.M. at the time the train was leaving the lower yard of Nacozari via the narrow gauge railway. All the employees jumped from the train except the locomotive engineer who remained aboard to prevent the train from rolling back and exploding in the lower yard.

"Explosion occurred at the moment the train entered the upper yard, in front of the section house. Eight women and children living in the section house, as well as five men, including the engineer, perished. They were all Mexican nationals except an American boy. Engineer was a native of Hermosillo and had worked on the same locomotive seven years. He died heroically."

Later in the day, Douglas wrote a letter to Governor Torres giving more details.

"There were 2,000 boxes of dynamite stored in the warehouse, and if the explosion had occurred there, the number of victims would have been frightening ... When the fireman yelled for him to jump, García answered by saying that if he did, the train might roll back toward the concentrator, and remained aboard the locomotive, intending, evidently, to reach the upper yard and run on through toward the mine in order to clear the section houses. His action was most heroic, for if indeed he had abandoned the train, it would have rolled back, and if the explosion had occurred at the bottom of the hill, the damages to the machine shop, stored powder, offices as well as the concentrator, would have been dreadful. The fireman and the brakemen also exhibited great courage in attempting to pull out the box of powder, which was smoking among the rest of the cargo, and in holding out until it started to burn. . ."

An article appeared in the *Douglas Daily International-American*:

"HEROISM OF MEXICAN SAVES NACOZARI
Deliberately Gave Up Life
In Performance of Duty.
Perished, With Fourteen Others, While
Taking Burning Train of Dynamite Out of Camp

"Long after the attendant horrors of yesterday's terrible explosion at Nacozari, when fourteen or fifteen lives were whiffed out, have been forgotten, and the bodies of the victims have crumbled into dust, the heroism of a Mexican engineer, Jesús García, who took the burning train, heavily laden with dynamite, out of the center of Nacozari, knowing that it would explode at any moment yet standing by his post in order to save the concentrator and other property in the city until death came to him, will be remembered–or should be. His matchless bravery and devotion to the highest conception of duty stands out in bold relief in the tragic occurrence of yesterday and will compare with any exploit in the annals of history."

This article appeared on page one of the Tucson, Arizona, *Star*, on November 9:

"ENGINEER'S BRAVERY SAVES MANY LIVES
He Tried to Get His Train Out of Town
To Prevent Explosion There

(Special to *The Star*)

"Nacozari, Nov. 8–That the concentrator and a good part of the town of Nacozari are not now in ruins is due to the bravery and heroism displayed by Jesús García, who was the engineer on the ill-fated train that was wrecked near here yesterday afternoon by the explosion of two cars of powder that were part of the train.

"The train consisted of four cars, the two nearest to the engine being open and loaded with powder. Two cars immediately behind these two were heavily loaded with baled hay. It was feared by the trainmen that owing to the size of the load some of the hay would topple off the cars. Consequently two bales were placed on the cars loaded with powder. A spark from the engine fell upon the hay and it was soon ablaze.

"The fireman, whose name could not be learned, looked back and noticed the blazing hay . . . cried to the engineer and begged him to jump from the train. The cars, however, were at that time just passing out through the town of Nacozari, and the engineer realized that if the explosion occurred near the town, a good part of the place would be destroyed and hundreds of lives lost. Realizing this, the brave man called to his fireman to jump, which the latter did, and the engineer then put on a full head of steam and started away from Nacozari. Owing to his quiet wit and wonderful display of nerve, the train was at least half a mile from the town when the frightful explosion occurred.

"The train at the time the powder exploded was passing through a small Mexican settlement and several houses which were located beside the track were blown to the ground, killing ten of the occupants . . ."

Jesús García's act of heroism has been memorialized by monuments erected in his honor at Pachuca, Guadalajara, Mazatlan, Naco, Aguas Calientes, Ciudad Obregon, Empalme, San Luis Portosi, and Tierra Blanca, and in Cuba, Guatemala, England, and Germany.

The most outstanding monument was erected in Nacozari with a $5,000 contribution from the Mexican government, along with monies from private citizens and the Moctezuma Copper Company honoring Jesús Garcia's incredible act of bravery.

My last conscious thought before finally falling asleep that evening in Nacozari was of the two-foot piece of jagged rail sailing through the air a distance of two miles and falling in the garden outside the guest house bedroom, and now resting on the mantel.

Jesús Garcia monument as it looks today, in the plaza at Nacozari (the town that Jesús saved).
Photo courtesy of Arizona Historical Society/Tucson. AHS# 75039

PANCHO VILLA'S SKULL

Coming in the next book! The intriguing true story of the disappearance of Pancho Villa's skull as told to me by my father.

Gen. Villa, as he fell across his car door, when killed.

Photo courtesy of Arizona Historical Society/Tucson. AHS# 29943

WHOSE FENCE?

Beginning at a mound of stones near the head of Aston Spring and on the north side thereof and near the edge of the Aston Spring Gulch...

The legal description of that part of the San Bernardino Land Grant lying within the United States fifteen miles east of Douglas, Arizona, is contained in a document recorded June 4, 1913, in Cochise County, Arizona.

The document also grants the U.S. government title to a strip of land sixty feet wide and lying immediately north of and parallel to the international boundary line.

In 1913, the boundary fence was nothing more than some loose barbed wires strung between crooked mesquite fence posts. The new U.S. fence, designed to help keep undocumented Mexicans out of the United States, does not yet extend as far east as the San Bernardino Ranch. The existing fence is made of six strands of barbed wire tightly strung between steel posts, with rigid wire stays between the posts.

On the southwest side of the ranch lies Silver Creek, a large, dry sand wash that runs under the boundary fence south to Mexico. During heavy rains, great amounts of flood water and flotsam are carried into the normally dry channel, washing away the fence.

In 1937, Granddad, Marion L. Williams, bought the San Bernardino from Viola Slaughter, John Slaughter's widow, who had been running the place since her husband's death.

Lying to the south of the San Bernardino, in Mexico, was a ranch owned by Dr. Calderón of Agua Prieta, Sonora.

Granddad and the good doctor had an understanding whereby they would exchange pertinent neighborly information and return stray livestock through a gate in the boundary fence. The gate belonged to the government, as did the lock placed thereon by U.S. Customs. Granddad had been given keys to the lock by U.S. Customs at Douglas, which provided easy access to his neighbor in Mexico.

The arrangement worked beautifully for a number of years until 1946, when a new group of officials took command at Douglas and changed the lock on the gate.

One Saturday morning in May, my cousin Tooter and I were at the ranch house in the front yard when Granddad tore through the gate as he returned from the border. He had told us earlier that he was on his way to the Calderóns to make arrangements to cross a mare and a young colt which had strayed onto the San Bernardino.

When he went to open the lock on the gate, his key wouldn't work. He tried and tried, without success, and upon looking more closely, saw that the lock had been changed. Nobody had informed him of the change, and the more he thought about it, the madder he got. He didn't stay at the ranch house long. He told Tooter and me he was going into town on business. We knew he was spittin'-nails mad.

Arriving at the customs office at the Douglas port of entry, he marched in, demanding to speak to the officer in charge. The officer, being new, did not recognize Granddad and became very officious when he was asked why the lock had been changed at the San Bernardino. Granddad also asked for a new key, explaining the arrangement he had with customs and the fact that he was permitted to have a key. He explained further that he used it only when necessary.

When he asked for the key, the officer responded, "Mr. Williams, that gate and fence are property of the United States government, as is the lock on the gate. You as a private citizen are not entitled to have a key and therefore you will not be given one. It is for the use of federal officers only."

Granddad once again explained to the officer his prior arrangement. The officer then reiterated his position. "Mr. Williams, we will not give you a key, and we are telling you to keep your hands off of that gate and fence. They are property of the United States government and you will be prosecuted if you tamper with them."

Infuriated at this, Granddad exploded. "You may be right about that gate and that particular piece of fence, but let me tell you one thing. In 1946 we had a big flood at Silver Creek that washed away a quarter mile of boundary fence into Mexico. I waited for the government to rebuild the fence, but nobody ever did, so I had my cowboys rebuild the damn thing. That part of the fence belongs to me, not the U.S. government."

"Well, Mr. Williams, let me tell you something. There is a sixty-foot strip of land along the north side of that boundary line which belongs to the U.S. government, and the fence you so graciously built now belongs to the United States government."

"Is that so? When I had my cowboys rebuild that fence, I had them rebuild it seventy feet north of the boundary line so that now, a quarter mile of that fence lies ten feet on my land, and the government doesn't have any damn right to the fence. Further, I'm going back to the ranch right now and tell the boys to tear the fence down, which will leave a quarter mile gap of open range between the U.S. and Mexico."

"Whoa, Mr. Williams, just a moment. I believe we can settle this amicably. If you will calm down a bit, we'll give you a key to the gate and you may use it at any time for your purposes."

Granddad was given the key. The two shook hands, and the matter was settled.

THE CATTALO EXPERIMENT

On February 21, 1941, Bill Greene, son of the well-known Col. W. C. Greene, founder of Cananea and its famous copper mines; Charles E. Wiswall, one-time manager of the Cananea Cattle Company and stepfather of W. C. Greene; A. J. Kalin, a wealthy landowner and cattle breeder from Brawley, California; Alfonso Morales, a well-established cattle rancher in northern Sonora; and Ben F. Williams, a cattleman residing in Cochise County; purchased the large Palomas Ranch located in Chihuahua, Mexico.

In addition to the 2,270,000 acres of land and 16,500 head of cattle, there came with the ranch a herd of fifty-five buffalo. They had been placed on the ranch in the "*cibola* pasture" by Edwin Marshall. He was an organizer of the Security First National Bank of Los Angeles, which owned the ranch at the time, and he had acquired title to the Palomas Land and Cattle Company.

Marshall and Henry S. Stephenson, an associate and subsequent owner of the operation, had the idea that by breeding Hereford bulls with buffalo cows, they would be able to create a new strain of hardy and heavy animals known as cattalo.

At the time when Dad and his partners purchased the ranch, the buffalo were well established in the cibola pasture. They had been there for a number of years and had multiplied through the breeding of buffalo bulls only to buffalo cows.

The ranch fence crew was kept busy repairing the pasture's fence, which

1943 photo of grand sire of buffalo herd, taken on Palomas Ranch

Ben F. Williams, Jr.

was frequently knocked down by the big, strong buffalo bull, the herd's sire. He weighed in at a ton. When he took a fancy to visit an adjacent pasture in order to find greener grass or a new girlfriend, he merely walked right through the barbed wire. You've heard the expression, "Strong as a bull." Well, he was.

Marshall and Stephenson had failed in their attempt to breed the new bovine animals which they hoped would be self-propagating. Although there were some animals born of the cross between the Hereford and the buffalo, those animals were like mules in that they did not produce progeny of their own.

From time to time, the Williams partnership slaughtered a yearling buffalo calf for consumption by the owners. I recall on one occasion being given the hide from one of the slaughtered calves. I kept it at my home in Douglas for a couple of years, until I finally decided to cut it into an oval-shaped rug to place at my bedside so as to have a warm place for my bare feet on cold mornings. At 4,000 feet elevation, Douglas got cold in the wintertime.

Two days after I cut my new bedside rug, Dad came home from his office in the Gadsden Hotel and told me he had been visiting with an Indian agent. They had discussed the herd of buffalo, and Dad told the agent I had the hide of a buffalo. The agent wanted to buy it.

I sadly related to Dad, "You know, I cut that hide up to make a rug just two days ago."

"That's a darn shame, because you could have sold it for $800."

Had I known that, rest assured I would not have cut it up!

The Williams group also attempted to cross the two species of stock, but without success.

In 1946, Ralph Morrow was an agent of the Arizona Fish and Game Commission in its enforcement division. He lived near Portal, Arizona. One day Dad and Ralph discussed the cattalo experiment, and Morrow said he also would also like to try cross-breeding Herefords and buffalo.

"Hell, Ralph, I'll give you a cattalo cow and you can experiment to your heart's content. We weren't successful in our efforts, but good luck to you."

Wanting to know more about Ralph's experiment, I recently contacted Wayne Morrow, Ralph's son, and asked him what he could tell me about the cattalo experiments.

Part of grand sire's harem, 1943, Palomas Ranch

Wayne wrote me a very interesting letter, saying among other things: "When your dad gave the cattalo to my Dad so many years ago, just prior to the foot-and -mouth fiasco closing the border, she was hauled out here in a one-horse trailer. She was a yearling at that time. . .she ranged over our country and most of the bordering ranches. So far as I know, she never hurt anyone but scared a few va- queros when they were branding or doctoring calves. Anytime a calf was roped within a quarter mile or so, she was right there, usually between the cowboy and his steed.

"She had a small tail similar to buffalo, which she lifted when upset–same as the buffalo. She grunted like a buffalo and while easy to handle, she was always at the outside of any bunch of cattle, letting you know she was not particularly

Two cows, granddaughters of Ralph Morrow's cattalo experiment,
on range near Portal, Arizona

pleased with matters. At around age four–just as the buffalo–she started producing calves. Again, they were like the buffalo in that most were red when young
and then turned black, or dark red.

"We used Hereford bulls, some polled, some horned. The only calf I remember
the cattalo producing with horns was a bull–very heavy and long-horned. He was
brown colored with dun-colored streaks down his sides. The Cave Creek dwellers
were always wanting a bull to breed to their milk cows and my dad thought he
would use this bull for that purpose, but after a few years he sold him. We raised
a number of bulls and some heifers with varying amounts of cattalo blood. All
were good producers. Our records show that calf weights at comparable ages were
greater than those with no buffalo blood. This may be partly due to higher butter
fat content. Buffalo milk has considerably more butter fat content than domestic
cattle. Also, the cows are thriftier and made better mothers.

"We sold some bulls to various ranchers. One bull we kept was out of the pet
cow, Evelyn. She was a gentle cow, but her offspring were not. This bull–we called

him Patch, though why Patricia named him so I do not know–was an exception. He had exceptional conformation and produced good calves. While I got along with him, some hands did not. He would break down fences, fight with any bulls he came across, and he became somewhat difficult to handle. He would run cowboys on horseback, and I always rode one of our good horses and had a double of rope ready when I was putting him back in the pasture. Anyway, Patch kept getting more rambunctious, and I was concerned that he might hurt someone."

Wayne shipped Patch to the auction at Willcox, where he was sold.

Continuing to comment on the experiment, Wayne wrote: "Looking at weight records, the smallest calf related to the cattalo we ever sold weighed over 400 pounds at five months. Weights usually ran over 500 to 600 pounds for six-to-seven-month-old calves. I believe a program of breeding for one-eighth to one-sixteenth buffalo blood would be an optimum cross and will produce superior beef cattle."

One of Wayne's last comments was: "The bull, Patch, was not too fat when sold but weighed over 1,800 pounds."

You might ask why the Morrow experiments were successful while the Marshall-Stephenson and Williams efforts failed. I really don't know. Do you have any ideas?

MEXICAN TAKEOVER

In 1941, the Williams-Greene group was negotiating to buy the Palomas Ranch located in Chihuahua, Mexico. It included 2,270,000 acres of land and 16,500 head of cattle. During negotiations, the buyers learned that former Mexican president Plutarco Elias Calles (1924-1928) had expropriated the ranch lands of the Palomas Land and Cattle Company by presidential decree.

Possession of the ranch by its former owners, however, was not affected by the decree because the takeover was never enforced by the Mexican government.

Prior to acquisition by the new buyers, a former owner, Henry S. Stephenson, had filed a claim for indemnification against the Mexican government for damages to the ranch arising out of the Mexican revolution (1910-1915). The claim was presented to and considered by the American-Mexican Claims Commission, which had been established to deal with cases where Americans whose property had been taken over or destroyed during the Mexican revolution were reimbursed for their losses.

At the time of purchase of the Palomas from Security First National Bank, the Williams group first learned of the cloud on title caused by the presidential decree and insisted that the claim be withdrawn by the law firm which had filed it for Stephenson, the former owner. This was made a condition of the purchase of the ranch by the buyers.

As it ultimately turned out, however, the claim was never withdrawn, and an offer of $1,660,000 was made to the heirs of Stephenson as indemnification for his losses by the commission.

One of the provisions of the law passed to indemnify damaged ranch owners was that monetary awards could be made only to American citizens. When the Williams-Greene partnership bought the ranch, it formed a Mexican corporation to act as buyer; the Mexican corporation didn't qualify for the award.

The Stephenson heirs, as individuals, did qualify, so the money involved in the settlement of the award was held in dispute. Litigation ensued, with a settlement made. The monies still owing to Security First National Bank were paid from the settlement proceeds. This satisfied the debt of the Williams-Greene partnership. Attorneys' fees were paid, with some money going to the Stephenson group and the balance to the Williams-Greene partners.

Once payment was made, the Mexican government took the position that the ranch had been "bought" by the government. No mention of reimbursement for revolutionary damages was made. By this time, Ben Williams had agreed with his partners to dissolve their partnership. For his part, Williams received the Buena Vista pasture, along with the south part of the "Los Moscos" pasture, both totaling

Las Palmas headquarters, looking north towards U.S.
Headquarters building on left, cowboy bunkhouse on right

Front view of Las Palmas headquarters

286,000 acres, along with twenty percent of all cattle and other personal property.

Carlos Serrano, president of the Mexican senate, claiming to act on behalf of the Mexican government, flew to Las Palmas (Williams' new ranch) in President Miguel Aleman's DC-3, along with two Mexican *pistoleros*. They landed on the airstrip I had previously built, two miles east of the Las Palmas headquarters.

Dad, Tom Ferrel (his ranch manager), and two Las Palmas vaqueros met the plane at the strip. Serrano confronted Williams, demanding the removal of his cattle–8,000 head of steers–and that he vacate the ranch. Williams was given six weeks to accomplish this.

Prior to the encounter with Serrano, Williams had been faced with the closing of the U.S. border by an embargo against the importation of Mexican cattle. This embargo was ordered on December 27, 1946, after an outbreak of foot-and-mouth disease had been reported. Some "infected" bulls were brought into Mexico at Vera Cruz–their place of origin was Brazil. A few of the bulls found their way into Texas, precipitating the border closure.

With the border closed, canneries were being built along the border to kill and process cattle which could no longer cross into the United States. One such processing plant was under construction in Juarez, across the border from El Paso.

Dad refused to move his cattle or surrender the ranch. It was only through the intervention of politically powerful friends in Mexico that he was able to forestall his eviction until the Juarez cannery was completed and could accommodate his needs.

He delivered 8,000 head for slaughter to the Juarez cannery, receiving only four and one-half cents per pound for his steers. The price of comparable cattle in the United States was a little over thirty cents per pound.

Once the cattle were gone, Dad abandoned Las Palmas, including the fine ranch house and all other improvements he had made.

I don't know who has the ranch today, and frankly, I don't care. What's that saying about crying over spilt milk?

MY DAD THE SMUGGLER
or
THE SECRET WEAPON

One afternoon when I was thirteen years old, living in Douglas, I came home from school to find a stranger in our back yard. He was dressed in khakis and sitting on a wooden box. There were three or four other boxes in front of him, all about fourteen inches square and six inches tall. The boxes contained crystals, each carefully wrapped in cotton and tissue paper. The crystals were clear and parallelogram in shape. Each easily fit in a man's hand. I asked the stranger what he was doing.

"I'm looking over some mineral specimens."

He obviously didn't want to talk, so I left.

Later that evening, when my father came home from work, I asked him who the man was and what he was doing. He said, "Oh, he's examining mineral specimens." He said no more, and I put it from my mind.

It was only in later years that I learned the whole story. Mom and Dad were at home one evening in 1942. I had already gone to bed when the phone rang.

Dad answered, "Hello."

"Is this Ben Williams in Douglas, Arizona?"

"Yes, it is."

"This is Captain Howard Noble calling from Washington, D.C., Mr. Williams. I am chief of procurement for the Army Air Corps."

"Captain, why are you calling me? I have nothing to do with the Air Corps."

69

"Maybe you do, and don't know it yet. Mr. Williams, can you go to the Douglas Army Air Base tomorrow and talk to Colonel Wadman, the base commander? He'll be expecting you."

"Oh, he will, will he?"

"Yes, and I'm sure you'll find it in your best interest to go see him tomorrow. I can't tell you any more on the phone. Thank you, Mr. Williams. Have a pleasant evening. Good night." With that, he hung up.

Dad wondered what the captain's call was all about. He barely slept that night. Early the following morning, he telephoned the base commander's office and made an appointment to see Colonel Wadman at ten o'clock. When he arrived at the colonel's office at the appointed time, his presence was acknowledged by Wadman's secretary, who immediately admitted Dad into his office.

After the usual courteous greeting, the colonel launched into a solemn statement.

"I have orders to fly you to Washington, D.C. I can tell you only that it is a secret mission of vital importance to our country. Beyond this, I can tell you nothing other than you are to meet a captain at the Pentagon."

"Colonel Wadman, I am not interested in going to Washington. I am very busy producing beef, which is critical to our country's war effort, and I don't have time for a trip to D.C."

"Mr. Williams, the Army Air Corps is interested in acquiring mineral crystals known as *Iceland spar*. The only known source was Iceland, and that source had dried up. You had better go see Captain Noble if you know what's good for you."

Not knowing what was behind the colonel's veiled threat, Dad reluctantly agreed to go. The government could cause him a lot of trouble at the border when he brought his cattle for importation into the United States.

Instead of flying, Dad took the train to Washington, where Captain Noble met him and took him to his office. He told Dad about the calcite crystals, saying there was a desperate need for them. They were a critical item needed for our war effort.

"Our government has found a deposit of optical calcite in a remote part of Chihuahua, but someone who is familiar with mining and Mexico is needed to facilitate bringing the crystals into the United States. The project is top secret. The calcite is used in a highly secret device by our military. No one is to know about the undertaking. Mr. Williams, we have investigated, and you are our man. We need your help."

"Captain Noble, what you are suggesting is smuggling those crystals out of Mexico and into the United States. I won't have anything to do with such an illegal act. It's a violation of our treaty with Mexico, in addition to being against the laws of both countries."

"Mr. Williams, the air corps is aware of that fact. You will be the person charged to get those crystals into this country. That is one reason we have picked you for the job. You have a reputation for knowing how to get things done."

"I can't lend myself to such a scheme, Captain."

"Mr. Williams, we know you are registered for the draft, and we have an infantryman's rifle just made to fit you should you refuse to help us."

"Since you put it that way, Captain, when do I start?"

"Right away. You will be supplied with whatever is required for the mission. A priority telephone number will be issued to permit you to make long distance calls to wherever you want without delay. What else will you need?"

"I'll need a specially equipped car with oversize wheels, tires, and springs, with a skid plate on the bottom and an oversize gas tank. The Mexican roads are washed out at times and hardly passable. Gas is hard to come by and stations are far apart. The car should be four-wheel drive, and the car's description and license plate circulated among U.S. customs so I can come and go without inspection or delay. It's important that my car pass through the border without inspection if this smuggling operation is going to succeed. The fewer people who know what I am carrying in my car or what I'm doing, the better."

"Don't worry, Mr. Williams, the border officers will be instructed to pass you and your car through without questions or inspection. The secrecy of our operation is essential and will be kept at all cost. Is there anything else you'll need?"

"I'll need a bank account to draw on. Of course, I'll account for all monies spent. Have your people contact me in Douglas.

"As you know, I own the electric power company in Agua Prieta, so the Mexican and U.S. border officers are used to seeing me daily when I'm not at the ranch in Chihuahua. The crystals will have to be put in forty-pound wooden boxes for ease of shipping. That way, they will fit in the trunk of my car.

"There will be a lot of other things that will arise, but we can take care of them as they come along. I'll have to go back and hire some Mexican miners to start. By the way, what is the calcite going to be used for?"

"I'm sorry, Mr. Williams, I'm not at liberty to tell you, other than it's critical to our war effort and everything about this is top secret."

"Okay, if you say so, Captain. I'll go back home and wait to hear from you."

"Right. It's a pleasure to meet you, Mr. Williams. I'm sure we have the right man for the job."

Dad returned to Douglas and made the necessary arrangements. The crystals were mined and brought to our back yard, where they were examined, hand graded, carefully packed in cotton and tissue paper, put into forty-pound wooden boxes and taken to the Douglas army air base for transport to some secret place.

By 1943, the calcite project was running smoothly. Crystals were being mined in Chihuahua; sorted; graded; packed; and shipped to Agua Prieta to Dad's electric utility, Compania de Servicios Publicos.

One evening, Angel Moreno, Dad's general manager, called him at home and informed him that he had received a load of wooden boxes consigned to Ben Williams at the company.

"I'll be over in the morning to pick 'em up," Dad told Moreno.

Early the next morning, Dad drove his car to Agua Prieta, where twenty boxes, each weighing forty pounds, were loaded into the trunk. It was riding at a rakish angle, with the rear end down and the front end up, much like a fast motor boat planing on a lake.

On his return to Douglas with the boxes in the trunk, Dad was stopped by a good friend, Dave Hopkins, the customs agent on duty at the port of entry, who was checking traffic.

"Good morning, Ben. How are you?"

"I'm fine, Dave, how are you?"

"Fine also. But Ben, what do you have in your car that's making it sit down so low in the back?"

"I'm sorry, Dave, I can't tell you."

"You can't tell me? Now, Ben, you know I'm an officer of the U.S. government and I can make you get out of that car and open the trunk."

Although they were good friends, Dave was doing his duty. The word was supposed to have been passed along the border to all customs officers so that when Dad appeared in his automobile, he was not to be stopped or questioned. The word hadn't reached agent Hopkins.

"I'm sorry, Ben. You're going to have to get out of the car and open the trunk."

Dad complied and opened the trunk to reveal the wooden boxes.

"Ben, what's in those boxes?"

"I'm sorry, Dave, I can't tell you."

"What do you mean?" Dave exploded. "I'll open every damn one of those boxes if I want to."

"No, Dave, I can't let you do that."

"Get out of the car and come inside the office," Dave commanded.

"Am I under arrest?"

"No, but your car is impounded."

Once inside the customs office, Dad asked if he could call a cab to go to his office.

"Yes, but the car stays here."

"Dave, don't open those boxes until I get back."

"Okay," Dave reluctantly replied.

Dad proceeded to the Gadsden Hotel where he placed a call to Captain Noble in Washington. During the war, it was extremely difficult to make long distance telephone calls. The lines were always busy, and frequently one had to wait for hours for a call to go through. However, Dad had been given a priority telephone number by Captain Noble and the operator immediately put his call through.

He told Captain Noble that he had been detained by customs at the border and his car impounded because he had refused to permit the customs agents to examine his cargo.

"Don't worry, Ben. I'll take care of the matter. You just stand by for a phone call."

Forty-five minutes later, Dad received a call from Mr. Specht, the officer in charge of the border at Douglas. He also was a friend of Dad's.

"Mr. Williams, come and get your car."

He had never previously addressed Dad as Mr. Williams, so Dad knew somebody in Washington had stirred the pot. He got into another cab at the Gadsden, went to the border, and entered the customs office to see Mr. Specht.

"Ben, I don't know what you've got in that damn car, and frankly, at this point, I don't care. You get in that car of yours and drive it out of here and don't look back."

Dad drove to the Douglas Army Air base nine miles north of Douglas, where the boxes containing the crystals were delivered to the base commander's office.

Things don't always work the way they're supposed to. However, glitches can be corrected, as was the case that morning. Dad had no idea where the crystals were destined to go.

Shortly after the war was over, Captain Noble called my father.

"Ben." (They had become well known to each other by that time.) "Ben, can you make arrangements to call on me the next time you are in Washington?"

"As a matter of fact, Captain, I'll be in New York in about two weeks. I can stop off in Washington on my way and see you."

Captain Noble met Dad in Washington and took him to his office. He closed the door and said, "Ben, I have never been able to explain to you what it was we were doing because it was of the very highest top-secret classification. I'll tell you now, however, that you were assisting us in obtaining optical calcite crystals which were used in the making of the Norden bombsight. It was the highly secret sight that permitted our Air Force to bomb and cripple Germany's war effort. It was also used to drop the atom bombs on Hiroshima and Nagasaki, bringing about Japan's early surrender. You can never be recognized by our government for what you have done. We can't give you a medal. The only thing that I can do, if you will permit me, is to ask you to have a drink with me."

"Of course."

Captain Noble reached into the bottom drawer of his desk and withdrew a bottle of Johnny Walker Black Label scotch, poured a generous portion for each of them, and toasted Dad.

Ben F. Williams, Jr.

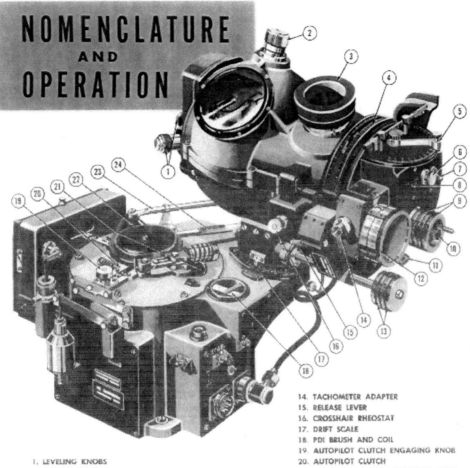

NOMENCLATURE
AND
OPERATION

1. LEVELING KNOBS
2. CAGING KNOB
3. EYEPIECE
4. INDEX WINDOW
5. TRAIL ARM AND TRAIL PLATE
6. EXTENDED VISION KNOB
7. RATE MOTOR SWITCH
8. DISC SPEED GEAR SHIFT
9. RATE AND DISPLACEMENT KNOBS
10. MIRROR DRIVE CLUTCH
11. SEARCH KNOB
12. DISC SPEED DRUM
13. TURN AND DRIFT KNOBS

14. TACHOMETER ADAPTER
15. RELEASE LEVER
16. CROSSHAIR RHEOSTAT
17. DRIFT SCALE
18. PDI BRUSH AND COIL
19. AUTOPILOT CLUTCH ENGAGING KNOB
20. AUTOPILOT CLUTCH
21. BOMBSIGHT CLUTCH ENGAGING LEVER
22. BOMBSIGHT CLUTCH
23. BOMBSIGHT CONNECTING ROD
24. AUTOPILOT CONNECTING ROD

The bombsight has 2 main parts, **sighthead** and **stabilizer**. The sighthead pivots on the stabilizer and is locked to it by the dovetail locking pin. The sighthead is connected to the directional gyro in the stabilizer through the **bombsight connecting rod** and the **bombsight clutch.**

Diagram of Norden bombsight as part of bombadier's kit

"You may not know it, but you saved thousands of lives by smuggling those crystals into this country, far greater than any contribution that you could ever have made as a rifleman. Ben Williams, I salute you!"

A CLASSY COUPE

In 1955, Dad special-ordered from General Motors a two-door Chevrolet coupe, color tan so that it would not show dirt and dust as he traveled throughout southern Arizona and northern Mexico on his mining and other businesses. At the time, Dad owned Compania Benwilco, a Mexican corporation which operated a copper and molybdenum mine southeast of Nacozari, Sonora.

Having traveled over the rough and treacherous roads of northern Mexico and southeastern Arizona, he knew he would have to have a vehicle that could handle the job. The car had to have an ample gasoline capacity because gas stations were few and far between. Also, at the smaller Mexican colonies, frequently the only pump in town was out of fuel, out of order, or without an attendant. Dad requested a Chevrolet with a 40-gallon-capacity fuel tank. That was a lot of gas for a car of the 1950s.

I recall one time when he pulled the Chevy up to the only ten-gallon hand-operated pump in Esqueda, a small Mexican community about forty miles south of Douglas. The tank was almost empty.

"*Favor de llenar mi caro*" (please fill my car), he instructed the station owner. The station was small. It consisted of a small grocery store with a gas pump out in front. The pump was the old-fashioned kind, with a metered ten-gallon glass container.

"*Si, como no*," responded the owner.

He proceeded to fill the car after pumping ten gallons of gas into the pump's measured glass container. The ten gallons went into Dad's car. A second ten gallons was then also put in after pumping the dispenser full once again. With twenty gallons in the vehicle, the owner once again filled his pump and emptied the fuel into the car. With thirty gallons in the auto, which was not yet full, the owner scratched his head and looked under the car to see where the leak was. No coupe he had ever fueled before had taken this amount of gas.

Ben F. Williams, Sr.; James Douglas (son of "Rawhide" Jimmy Douglas, brother of Lewis Douglas, U.S. Ambassador to the Court of St. James during FDR's administration); and Mrs. Douglas; in cut of road showing Dad's custom-built coupe

"Que pasó?" (What happened?) inquired the attendant.

"Tiene tanque grande," said Dad. *"Lleva cuarenta galones."* (It has a big tank. Takes forty gallons.)

"Oh, muy bien."

Seven more gallons, and we were off once again.

Other unique features of the car included a heavy metal skid plate which extended under the radiator, oil pan, transmission, and fuel tank to protect them from striking boulders and high centers on country roads, and oversized radiator that provided enough coolant for the engine to prevent overheating.

The water, carried in the large Desert brand, heavy canvas bag on the outside of the car door, was used for both drinking and radiator. As long as the car was moving, evaporation on the bag kept the water cool for drinking even when the weather was hot, as was usually the case in the Sonoran Desert of the Southwest. In those days, four-wheel-drive transmissions had not yet been introduced for civilian use in passenger cars, so the Chevy was two-wheel drive. Oversized wheels, tires and springs were installed to further elevate the chassis to protect against high centering.

Both Arizona and Sonora license plates were affixed to the car to facilitate border crossing and its use in both the U.S. and Mexico. The purchase of Mexican plates required that import duties be paid to Mexican tax authorities. The duties in those days equaled 110 percent of the U.S. purchase price of the vehicle–no small amount, but worth its value for the use made of the car. (Cost of the car: $10,000. Cost of Mexican plates: $11,000.)

After ten years of faithful service, the car finally succumbed to the rough country roads and was put to rest in the auto boneyard.

GRINGO

Have you ever been to Warren, Arizona, near Bisbee? If so, you may have noticed that the sidewalks and curbs are stained a muddy brown color. This was caused by many years of watering plants, trees, and lawns with mine water–water containing a high mineral content that flowed out of the tunnels of the copper mines at Bisbee. The mine's water was used to process copper concentrates. The waste water was then dumped into the tail ponds.

Trees, plants, shrubs, and lawns in Warren were always greener than in other towns. This caused my father to wonder what it was in the mine water that made plants greener, so he sent a sample of the water to a laboratory for analysis. The lab analysis showed a high iron content and a great number of trace elements.

In those days, you could buy iron fertilizer or soil supplements from most flower shops and nurseries. It was expensive, however.

With this in mind, Dad experimented by applying the mine water to other areas. When the mine water was added to the usual irrigation waters, foliage became greener.

Wondering if increasing the iron content in the product might make the foliage yet more green, he experimented more. Sure enough, plants grew faster and greener.

Dad's idea was to percolate mine water through the tail ponds, thereby concentrating the liquid. This pregnant liquor was captured below the tail ponds and

81

PAT. NO:3,135,395

MINERAL SULPHATE
SOIL ACID SOLUTION

United States Patent Office

761,200
Registered Dec. 10, 1963

PRINCIPAL REGISTER
Trademark

Ser. No. 142,948, filed Apr. 24, 1962

GRINGO

Iron Products, Inc. (Arizona corporation)
P.O. Box 1051
Douglas, Ariz.

For: FERTILIZER, in CLASS 10.
First use Mar. 23, 1962; in commerce Mar. 23, 1962.

run into a cement tank which contained scrap iron and tin cans.

The rectangular tank had to be constructed with cement containing special sand because the water was highly acidic and ate through the silica in river sand normally used to make concrete.

By introducing iron into the tank containing the pregnant liquor (copper sulfate), a leaching process began. The leaching is similar to what we learned about in high school chemistry. Iron in solution is displaced by copper in the process. The iron goes into solution and copper falls to the bottom of the tank in the form of sludge. The sludge is almost pure copper and goes to the smelter where it is smelted like other copper concentrates.

The highly concentrated copper water was exposed to iron, in the form of scrap and tin cans. Tin cans had a high content of iron, being more satisfactory for leaching than heavier iron. However, any iron would suffice. Sulfuric acid was added to enhance and quicken the leaching process.

Now we had iron sulfate–sulfate from the copper sulfate, and iron from the tin cans. This iron sulfate was applied to crops. Where the product was used in growing fields of corn, the rows of corn where the product had been added grew a couple of feet higher and were greener than the rows of corn immediately adjacent, where no product had been applied.

Allan Hood, a Douglas resident and friend of Dad's, became interested in the project and invested, becoming one of the principal owners. I formed an Arizona corporation, which we called Iron Products, Inc. Dad filed an application for a U.S. patent for the leaching process. I'll be darned if a patent wasn't granted. It's hard to believe that the classic process of leaching copper and iron had never been patented, although the general concept had been in use for many years.

Allan, Dad, and I felt we needed a catchy name for the product. We decided to name it "Gringo." That's what Mexicans have called Anglos for many years. Legend has it that the name was derived because of a song Americans sang in Texas in the 1920s. It went something like, "Green grow the lilacs, oh!" Mexicans began calling Anglos "gringos."

I wondered if the word "gringo" could be trademarked or copyrighted. I contacted a law firm in Washington, D.C., and as a consequence of their efforts, the word "Gringo" was granted as U.S. trademark serial number 142,948 for our product.

We began producing Gringo in commercial quantities at our plant site at Bisbee. We sold the product to citrus growers in California, who found that it prevented what they called "early drop," a condition where the fruit dropped from the trees before maturity.

Bud Antle Farms at Marana, Arizona, purchased great quantities of Gringo, which we sold in tank car lots. They found it beneficial for the lettuce they grew. Bud Antle Farms was well known in the Tucson area, and their lettuce was sold throughout the United States. Antle's offices were in the old Westerner Hotel in Tucson.

We also dehydrated the liquid product to reduce it to powder form. This was sold as a fertilizer in flower shops and nurseries.

Further experimentation in applying the powder to livestock feed produced greater weight gain of feeder cattle. Some of the dried product was sold to Arizona Colorado Land and Cattle Company. The cattle at first wouldn't eat it because of its pungent taste, but after it was sprayed with molasses they really ate it up, greatly increasing their weight gain.

Dad got some number two empty gelatin capsules from Arizona Drug and filled them with this dry Gringo powder. He took one capsule a day for years and swore they made him feel good, better than multipurpose vitamins, because Gringo contained all the trace elements needed for good health.

On January 19, 1972, we sold the company with all rights to Arizona-Colorado Land and Cattle Company of Phoenix.

Guess it really pays to look at "muddy" sidewalks and wonder why.

GOOD OL' BOYS

THE GRIZZLY BEAR

Sighting in on the bear with my rifle, I thought, *Now how much elevation should I allow for three hundred yards?*

That bear was a huge grizzly that had been terrorizing the neighborhood for a long time. He had broken into five cabins and raised havoc, tearing up furniture and cupboards looking for food. When he stood up on his hind feet and extended his front legs, he measured a good eight feet and weighed God only knows how much.

I had been looking for him off and on for several weeks and finally had him in the scope of my .300 Savage rifle. The country was wooded, but he was in an open spot grazing on wild raspberries.

Grizzlies have been known to rip off the top of a man's skull with a single blow. They are powerful beyond belief, and although it seems as though they can only lumber along at a slow pace, they run incredibly fast when provoked.

I finally had the big guy in my gunsight and was going to rid the country of this menace. Figuring that two clicks elevation on the sight would do it for distance, I carefully turned the knob two clicks, and the barrel raised to what I thought was the proper elevation. Just as I was getting a clear sight in the crosshairs on the heart of that devil, a breeze came up over my left shoulder. Now, I must adjust also for windage.

At three hundred yards, I figured it would take three clicks to the right to handle the breeze. When this adjustment was made, I looked again through the scope, and just as I was drawing a bead on the beast, some crows flew overhead, squawking, and spooked that darned bear.

Startled by the birds, the bear stood straight up, looked in my direction and quickly bolted into the nearby woods, not to be seen again.

My vision of a beautiful bearskin rug in front of my fireplace vanished along with the bear.

I put the gun sling over my shoulder and walked back to camp, feeling completely defeated.

There would be another day, and another opportunity to settle the score with Mr. Grizzly.

HUNTING LICENSE

As he looked through the periscope of his Sherman tank out over the skyline in the winter of 1944, searching for German Tiger tanks, Shelley Richey[1] glanced above the viewfinder for a quick look at an official notice which he had received at mail call the previous day. He had read the notice aloud to the men of his command, who thought it was hilarious, so much so that they took the document and pasted it in the turret of Shelley's tank.

He was on active duty with an armored unit which had for two weeks been heavily engaged in running gun battles with a crack German tank battalion. The Germans were equipped with the deadly "Tiger tanks," which were superior to our Shermans. Their armor plate was heavier than ours and many of our tankers reported that the shells from our 76-millimeter cannons merely bounced off the Tigers' turrets, while the German 88-millimeter tubes wreaked havoc when their projectiles hit our tanks. They penetrated our armor plate, sending deadly fragments flying around inside our medium tanks.

The fighting had been fierce, with Shelley's unit advancing so fast during the previous three weeks that it had run out of fuel and ammunition. Without gas and ammo, his battalion, which was the spearhead of Patton's Third Army, had come to a halt and was taking a well-deserved rest in some woods in the Alsace-Lorraine hills while waiting for needed supplies. During the lull, their mail caught up with them outside Nance, France.

---

1 Shelley Richey practiced law in Douglas for many years until he moved to Tucson where he practiced for a few years before retiring. He is now 92 years of age and still has a very clear and acute mind. Many of the details from this story were garnered from a personal interview at Shelley's home on August 30, 2008.

The piece of paper that Shelley now glanced at read, "Official Notice. You are hereby notified that your hunting rights have been restored. This is an official notice from the State of Arizona Game and Fish Department. You may hunt, subject to current regulations, immediately upon receipt of this document."

Shelley thought, *Whoopee! Now it's legal for me to hunt those damn Germans!*

He recalled the previous day at mail call, when the company mail clerk announced, "Lieutenant W. Shelley Richey, here's something for you. It looks official."

Reading the notice again, Shelley recalled how he had lost his "hunting rights." He and his hunting buddy, Joe, had set out early on an October morning in 1942 for the old Willow Springs Ranch northeast of Oracle Junction back in Arizona (a ranch which coincidentally had been owned by my grandfather, Marion Williams, from 1932 until 1937). Joe and Shelley had jumped a covey of Gambel quail and left their car parked on the side of a dirt road before chasing after the wily birds. The road was well established, with a considerable amount of traffic. They had hiked the hills chasing the covey without much luck, although Shelley could occasionally hear the report of Joe's shotgun. Shelley became tired and returned to the car. He had barely sat down in the shade of the automobile when up jumped a big animal not fifty feet in front of him. He quickly grabbed the shotgun, fired, and the animal dropped.

At about the same time, a pickup truck pulled up and parked behind Shelley's car. A man got out and approached, inquiring, "Howdy. What's going on?"

"Well, I've been quail hunting with my pal Joe. I got tired and came back to the car and sat down when just now a big deer jumped up and I shot him. I haven't even gone over to see him yet. He's lying over there not fifty feet from here in that little swale."

"Oh, is that right? What did you shoot him with?"

"With this shotgun. It used to belong to my father."

"Oh? You mind if I look at it?"

"Sure. Here." Shelley handed the 12-gauge Winchester pump to him.

"Oh, this is a beauty," the stranger said as he cranked the pump, ejecting five shells. "I notice that you don't have a plug in the gun."

"That's right, I guess."

"Oh? And you shot that deer with this gun?"

"Yes."

"Let's go take a look." They went to the low swale and sure enough there was a big animal lying dead on the ground.

The man said, "That was a fine shot, but I gotta tell you, I'm the game warden, and you have just shot an antelope out of season. Let me see your license."

Shelley said, "It's back in the car."

"Well, I gotta tell you something else, sir. You just illegally shot from the side of a road, which is prohibited by law, with a shotgun loaded with bird shot, which is against the law. You shot an antelope out of season with a shotgun that does not have a plug limiting the number of shells to three. I'm sorry, sir, but I've got to cite you and take your gun. Also, I've got to confiscate the antelope as prescribed by law and deliver it to the proper authorities."

The Game and Fish Department took the antelope and disposed of it.

Shelley wound up in the justice court at Florence, the county seat of Pinal County where the infractions occurred.

Just a few days after Shelley's attorney had successfully handled his case, reducing the charges down to one, with a fine of three hundred dollars, Shelley received an official notice from the Arizona Game and Fish Department informing him that his hunting privileges had been suspended indefinitely because of the violations.

Upon receiving the reinstatement of his hunting privileges, Shelley's men pasted the notice above the gun sight of his 76-millimeter cannon in the tank.

As he looked through the viewfinder of his tank, he thought to himself, *Well, I guess it's all right now to hunt Germans.*[2]

---

2 After receiving his official notice from Arizona, for three days and nights during the winter campaign against the Germans, Shelley directed artillery fire while hidden in a bunker that was part of the old Maginot Line. For this action, Shelley was awarded a Bronze Star for bravery and heroism above and beyond the call of duty. After the Battle of the Bulge, Shelley received yet another Bronze Star for bravery and gallantry in action and a Silver Star, along with a battlefield promotion, for successfully defending a bridge as rear guard while U.S. troops withdrew, providing time for our engineers to blow it up and keep the Germans from crossing the river.

ANCHORS "AWAY!"

Bill Kimble was Superior Court judge of Cochise County for several years. He enjoyed fishing at Lake Angostura, seventy miles south of Douglas. Angostura was one of my favorite fishing holes as well. Bill has some great stories to tell about that spot.

He had a good friend, Joe Saba, a prominent physician and surgeon employed by Phelps Dodge corporation in Bisbee. Joe, a great guy and lots of fun, owned a fourteen-foot boat which he pulled on a trailer behind his pickup. The rig was ideally suited for travel to and fishing in the good bass-fishing Mexican lake. The boat was equipped with an outboard motor to propel it around, although not at any great speed.

In June 1971, Joe asked Bill and another friend, Vince Burns, who was school superintendent at Bisbee, to accompany him for a weekend of large-mouth bass fishing. Bill never did profess to be much of a fisherman, but he claimed he had "drowned" a goodly number of worms while attempting to perfect his fishing technique. Vince knew little, if anything, about fishing and boating, but he was a happy companion to have along on a fishing trip.

Angostura Lake is large–eighteen miles long and three miles wide at its widest point. It is named "angostura" because the dam is built between two high perpendicular rock bluffs which are located in close proximity to each other in a narrow canyon. Thus, the name "angostura" (translated, the narrows).

After arriving at the lake and a good evening's rest and fine breakfast, the three set out in Joe's boat in quest of large-mouth bass. The lake is known for being very turbulent at times because of strong winds that suddenly come up, often causing boats to capsize. A number of people have drowned during such storms. I have been on the lake several times when sudden storms came up and whipped the lake into a frothy frenzy. In those times, the prudent boatman would head his boat to a quiet cove until the winds had subsided and the turbulence abated.

Our three fishermen found themselves in such a situation at mid-afternoon.

"Fellows, we'd better get off this blasted lake and find a quiet cove to wait out this thunderstorm," Joe announced.

Spotting a good cove, he skillfully guided the boat into the quieter waters and hollered above the din of the storm to Vince, who was in the bow, "Throw out the anchor!"

Vince followed Joe's instructions to the letter. He grabbed the anchor, which was attached to a rope, and threw both over the front end of the boat. His companions watched horrified as the anchor and rope sailed far out into the water.

Next could be heard a loud "plop." Immediately thereafter, Joe–who was never bashful–screamed, "Vince, you damn fool! Didn't you tie the end of that rope to the boat?"

"No. You didn't tell me to. I threw it over as instructed."

There followed a barrage of language, most of which is unprintable here, spewing from Joe's mouth.

After a while, the storm and tempers subsided, and the crew returned to camp to enjoy a few libations to soothe their frayed nerves.

The last words anybody could remember being uttered were, "Vince, who the hell taught you anything about boating?"

"Joe, I'm a fisherman, not a boater," responded Vince.

The anglers returned to Bisbee with their catch of several bass in the three-to-five-pound class, caught before the storm.

Is there a moral to the story? Indeed there is. When you hear the command, "Anchors aweigh," be dang sure the anchor rope is tied at both ends.

THE SWAMPER

George Swanson, Gordon Newman, Jr., and I had decided to go fishing at Lake Angostura. We left Douglas and Agua Prieta about four o'clock one Thursday afternoon after obtaining our visas and vehicle permit. Along with our fishing gear and groceries, we had stashed away a pretty good amount of booze to enjoy on our long fishing weekend.

At the Agua Prieta immigration office was a young man about twenty-five years old whose name was Rogelio. He was the person who placed the automobile *permiso* (permit) stickers from Mexican customs on our windshield. Of course, we had to pay him a couple of dollars gratuity for his services.

While Rogelio was affixing our sticker, one of the Mexican customs officers told me that Rogelio was a good swamper who could help around camp, loading and unloading our boat and equipment. He could also cook, wash dishes, and take care of any other chores that might be required.

I told George and Gordon about Rogelio's talents. We all thought it was a good idea to have a helper go with us, so we engaged him.

On arrival at the fishing lodge, we unloaded our personal and camping gear and put the boat in the water to be ready go fishing early the next morning. Fishing had been reported to be excellent, and large-mouth bass of three to five pounds were being caught with water dogs. In the early mornings, top water plugs were the fish's favorites.

On our first evening in camp, we enjoyed some prime charcoal broiled steaks, along with french fries, canned peas, and rolls for dinner. This we topped off with sliced peaches and chocolate cookies for dessert. Rogelio washed the dishes and tidied up the camp while my fishing companions and I told each other tall tales until bedtime.

After a good night's rest, we awoke early the next morning to the delightful aroma of freshly brewed coffee, courtesy of Rogelio. He had fixed us a hearty breakfast of bacon, eggs, toast, and coffee, which we wolfed down. There's something about fishing and camping that always makes for a good appetite.

Author at Nacozari Lake fishing camp

Author and Mike Vasquez, along with Rogelio (swamper) and two extra passengers

At the water's edge, Rogelio helped us load our fishing gear into the boat. This included a small ice chest in which was carefully packed ice, beer, and juices. A bottle of Canadian V.O. was also on ice. Fishing rods and tackle boxes were placed in the boat for easy access.

I told Rogelio we would be back late in the afternoon and asked him to prepare some french fries and heat up the stew we had brought from home in a pressure cooker. Then off we went, with Rogelio waving us "adios."

After a fine day of fishing, during which we caught thirty-five bass averaging two to three pounds each, we headed back to camp hungry as wolves, thirsty as camels, and ready for a fine round of drinks and dinner.

Arriving back at camp, we found all the booze gone and Rogelio weaving around trying to look like a cook. He had made french fries, all right. They were scattered all over the ground where he had spilled them. Rogelio was in the process of trying to heat the stew when we assumed command and told him to go somewhere and sleep it off. We prepared our dinner, such as it was, then retired.

When we awakened early the next morning, there was no smell of fresh coffee and no trace of Rogelio. Knowing that he was in bad odor, Rogelio had left camp during the night, never to be seen again.

WANDERING SIX-SHOOTER

Tom Hood, Floyd Kimble, Charlie Bloomquist, and my father, Ben Williams, shared office space in the Gadsden Hotel. The office was close to the main hotel entrance.

One day Tom decided to run for sheriff of Cochise County. He secured the required petitions, circulated them, obtained enough signatures, and filed them to qualify as a candidate for office. He was not able to campaign a great deal because of his work schedule. Tom was a bookkeeper who took care of accounting for a large number of cattlemen and ranchers.

Tom was well known in and around Douglas, but in the far reaches of Cochise County few people knew him.

Come election day, Tom showed poorly. The day after the election, he was seen walking the streets of Douglas wearing a six-shooter, which he had never done before.

One of his friends stopped him. "Tom, since when did you start wearing a six-shooter?"

"Since I learned just how few friends I have during yesterday's election."

WENDY'S SUBMARINE

Wendell (Wendy) Spence was my neighbor in Douglas for a number of years. The Spences lived directly across the street from me. He was my barber, as well as a good friend. Every couple of weeks, I went to his shop in the Gadsden Hotel to reap the benefits of his tonsorial talents. The shop was located next to the front entrance on "G" Avenue.

Wendy had purchased Bob Poston's 14-foot aluminum fishing boat, along with a 7 ½-horsepower Johnson outboard motor and homemade boat trailer. He rigged it with a removable canvas shade to protect against the burning sun when fishing in the summer. It was not a very pretty rig, but it was practical.

I was seated in Wendy's barber chair one day when he told me of his most recent fishing trip to Angostura. Before he and a friend left Douglas for the lake, they loaded a lot of equipment, groceries, and booze into his truck.

He and his companion arrived at the lake in the late afternoon. On the way, they had partaken of a number of drinks. On arriving, they unloaded the truck, put all of the cargo into Wendy's boat, and climbed aboard to ferry over the fifty yards of water to the east shore, where they would establish their camp.

Wendy was in the nose of the boat and his friend was operating the motor. As the boat left the shore, Wendy hollered, "I think we've overloaded the boat. It's sitting real low in the water and the nose is going to go under. Oops! There she goes!"

Wendy's submarine, purchased by author after
its maiden underwater voyage

Indeed the nose submerged, just like a submarine, taking with it all the gear, plus Wendy, his friend–and the remaining booze!

They were able to swim to shore after the boat sank. Help was needed to recover the boat and motor. Although they got most of their gear, some was left on the bottom of the lake.

The moral of the story: Don't go boating when you're "overloaded."

HOW FAR TO WATCHICAMPO?

We had all been looking forward to a good large-mouth bass fishing trip to Lake Angostura, seventy miles south of Douglas in Mexico. Angostura Dam backs up the waters of the Bavispe River for a distance of eighteen miles, and at its widest it is three miles across. Nineteen hundred sixty-four was a wet year, and the lake was full. Recent reports told of excellent top water action.

Five of us had carefully loaded our two pickups with fishing gear and boats. Dr. Robert (Bosco) Montgomery, a local physician and surgeon from Douglas, George A. Swanson, western comptroller of Phelps Dodge Corporation, and I were in the cab of the lead pickup, which was driven by Bosco, a native of Louisiana and graduate of LSU Medical School. Bosco had finally figured out how to speak Spanish, having lived and practiced medicine in Douglas since the Second World War.

It was September and the monsoon rains had passed, so the dirt roads were again passable. Our 14-foot aluminum fishing boat was well fastened to a rack on top of the pickup. In the second pickup were Shelley Richey, a lawyer from Douglas, and Frank Fair, owner of a sporting goods store in town. They trailed a fourteen-foot bass tracker boat.

We cleared customs and immigration at Agua Prieta. South of town, we passed through the secondary checkpoint at kilometer 47, after which there were no further inspection stations to hinder our travel. The *garrita* (checkpoint) at kilometer 47 was nothing more than an unfinished adobe building by the side of the road, with the customary *"Alto"* (stop) sign in front. The inspection at kilometer 47 was as usual very perfunctory and as always made less troublesome by a couple of ice-cold beers provided by us for the inspecting officers.

The next point of interest was Fronteras, a small Mexican pueblo. Its history reached back as far as early frontier days when the Spaniards established a presidio in what they called the *pimeria alta*. We sailed through town on a dirt road without stopping.

Then on to Esqueda, where a mining company known as Fluor Esqueda was milling and stockpiling fluorspar, a critical mineral used by

Shelley Richey, Frank Fair, and author, before departing for Watchicampo

the U.S. in our space program. There were two small *mercados*, a *cantina* with a billiard table, and one lone gas pump in the community. Of course, it had a church and school and boasted a population of 350.

It was our custom to stop for a Carta Blanca beer at the cantina. Cowboys tied their horses to a hitching rail at the front door before entering for a cool one and a game of billiards. A few cowboys played, while a number watched. This was a great place for a drink to settle the dust in our throats, for we had been on the rough dirt road for an hour.

Now, as I said earlier, Bosco had mastered the Spanish language. He figured that the only thing he had to do was to put an "o" on the end of each word in order to speak like a native. For example, when asked by the barkeep if he would like another beer, he said, *"No gracias, yo have-o."*

The barkeep smiled, understanding every word spoken by the good doctor.

The next leg of the trip took us to a small pueblo which maintained a flat clearing where the local inhabitants played baseball every Sunday afternoon. This little pueblo was known as Turicachi. Stone breastworks overlooked the community from the surrounding hills. They had been built and manned by government troops during the days of the Mexican revolution. Pancho Villa's troops passed through Turicachi after a gun battle to the south with the *federales* in Nacozari while on their way to capture Agua Prieta in 1915. It should be noted that Villa was not successful in his quest.

Once out of Turicachi on our way to the upper waters of Lake Angostura, where the Bavispe River flowed into the reservoir, there were no further settlements other than an occasional ranch house reached by dirt trails that branched off our one-lane road.

By the side of the road as we left Turicachi stood a young man holding a large bandana containing undisclosed personal items. He waved to flag us down, and Bosco stopped the truck. In his perfect Spanish, Bosco asked the young man, *"Que you need-o?"*

The man clearly understood and immediately responded, *"Watchicampo."*

A good day's catch at Watchicampo

"Bueno. Que es su name-o?" (Good. What is your name?)

"Jesús."

George and I were fascinated by this exchange of fluent Spanish but said nothing. Bosco motioned for the young man to jump in the back of the pickup, which he did, and off we motored again. We passed a number of side roads and two or three little ranch houses, but the young man in the back of the truck never uttered a word.

Bosco said, "I guess he'll tell us when we get to the turnoff to Watchicampo."

George and I nodded our heads in agreement as we proceeded. After a while, Bosco said, "Do you suppose we've passed the turnoff to Watchicampo and the guy in the back has just been too timid to tell us to stop?"

George and I said nothing, for we could readily tell that Bosco was in complete control of the situation. After traveling a few more kilometers, I said to my friends, "He'd better tell us pretty soon where the cutoff to Watchicampo is because we're almost at the lake."

Bosco said, "Do you suppose we passed it?" George and I were puzzled but made no comment.

Finally, Bosco turned to me and said, "Benny, you speak Spanish a little better than I do. I'm going to stop and you ask that guy where Watchicampo is."

He stopped. I got out and inquired of our rider, *"Donde está Watchicampo? Ya hemos pasado el camino a Watchicampo?"* (Where is Watchicampo? Have we passed the road to Watchicampo?)

"Oh, no, señor."

Then he proceeded to tell me in Spanish that when first addressed by Bosco, he thought he was asking him what he wanted, and he had said in his best English "watchicampo," meaning "may I watch your camp?" Bosco, of course, thought "Watchicampo" was the name of a pueblo or colony and assumed that Jesús would tell us when we got there.

When I related to my companions what Jesús had said, they declared, "Well, let's go ahead and take him and he can be our watchicampo. It's too far to take him back."

Jesús helped unload our gear, washed the dishes, cleaned our catch, and did all the other things that go with a fishing camp.

We found our watchicampo so helpful that we thereafter always looked for a watchicampo to take with us on our forays into Mexico.

THANKS FOR THE MEMORIES

(MOST OF 'EM ANYWAY)

PEARL HARBOR DAY

How well I remember Pearl Harbor Day. My uncle, Morris Browder, was operating the windlass at his manganese prospect ten miles southeast of Safford. He and a friend, Doug MacGregor, were partners in the manganese prospect and had been following a promising vein for some time. They had dug a shaft fifty-five feet deep, and every Sunday they would continue to dig, hoping the vein would enlarge and "enrich at depth," as the miners say.

A stovepipe had been installed from the surface to the bottom of the shaft. On the surface was attached a blower such as is used by blacksmiths for blowing air. This device provided fresh air for whoever might be working in the bottom of the shaft.

On that particular Sunday, December 7, a Mexican man was digging in the bottom of the mine while Morris operated the windlass and Doug operated the blower.

I was twelve years old and had been hunting with my .410 shotgun. Rabbits and quail had escaped me all morning. I had not been able to bag anything. About 9:30, I was tired and sat down in the car to rest. I turned on the radio and heard the announcement that Pearl Harbor had been bombed by the Japanese, there were unknown numbers of casualties, many ships had been damaged or sunk, and a number of aircraft had been damaged or destroyed, both on the ground and in the air. It was a surprise attack and in Honolulu the radio announcers were extremely excited in their reporting.

Hearing the awful news, I immediately ran to Uncle Morris and Doug Mac-Gregor at the mine shaft opening and told them of the bombing. Even though I was young, I realized it was extremely bad news. Soon thereafter, Franklin Delano Roosevelt announced the declaration of war on Japan and mobilization began in the United States.

My cousin Hector enlisted in the army air corps and served during the entire war as a radio operator after he trained at Randolph Field in San Antonio.

I recall vividly many Boy Scout drives I participated in, going throughout the city of Douglas gathering lead-based toothpaste tubes, rubber items of all types, string, newspapers, and other scraps that could be used in our war effort. The lead from the toothpaste tubes was used to make bullets, and the rubber was reprocessed and used in retread tires.

I also remember rationing–stamps for food and gasoline.

Mother was in Douglas on the day of the attack and Dad was at the Palomas ranch in Chihuahua.

Oh, what a horrible feeling it was to realize that we had been violated, particularly after the Japanese envoys had been in Washington trying to convince our government and state department that they were friends and would continue to be friends forever.

I remember so well the many slogans, such as, "A slip of the lip can sink a ship."

What a terrible time! I hope we never have to go through such an ordeal again, but I know the American people can handle it if required.

NUMBER, PULEEZE

My home had been in Douglas for all my life except the two last years of high school when I attended New Mexico Military Institute. Now it was September 1947 and I was off to the University of Arizona.

In those days, the telephone switchboard for Douglas was located in Bisbee, some twenty-two miles west of Douglas. In order to call Douglas, you had to place your call through the Bisbee operator.

Our home phone number was "78," quite a difference from today's ten-digit numbers. In those days, when you lifted the receiver, an operator came on line and asked, "Number, puleeze."

"I want to place a call to Douglas, Arizona."

"Just a moment puleeze while I connect you with the Bisbee operator."

After a brief pause, I would hear, "This is the Bisbee operator. How may I help you?"

"This is Ben Williams, Jr., calling Ben Williams at 78 in Douglas, person-to-person collect."

"I'm sorry, but the Williamses are not home this evening."

"Do you know where they are, operator?"

"They've gone to supper with the Warners. They're at the Club Top Hat."

In a small town like Douglas in the 1940s, everyone knew everyone else's business. Also, if you were expecting a phone call, you could call the operator and give her your itinerary.

"Thank you, operator. Can you please ring that number?"

"Just a moment, puleeze."

Then she would ring the Top Hat and ask for Ben Williams.

"Mr. Williams, I have a collect call from your son in Tucson. Will you accept the charges? Shall I bill your home phone?"

"Yes, operator, I'll accept the call." Then Dad and I would talk.

What a wonderful innovation it was when we got a new phone with a rotary dial and were able to dial direct from Tucson to Douglas–a sad thing for the Bisbee operator, however. She was no longer needed. Also sad because rotary dial never knew one's whereabouts.

I also recall that before direct, ten-digit dialing, to speak to someone in Douglas, you would say, "Operator, I want to speak with Empire," and then the number. "Empire" was the Douglas prefix.

Then came a change to direct-dial calling. As the state grew, area codes became necessary to handle the increased telephone traffic. Area codes, as we know today, are often changed in order to accommodate our dynamic growth.

Well, I guess we have to keep up with the changes although it sure was nice to know where and how to get in touch with someone in those days of fewer telephones.

GADSDEN HOTEL

How would you like to have your office in the Gadsden Hotel in Douglas, Arizona?

On October 13, 1956, when I first started to practice law, my office there was off the north door of the lobby. In the wintertime, some of the coldest air ever felt came off Eleventh Street into that hotel through that door. Dad–Ben F. Williams, Sr.–had paid for the remodeling of the small office, which we shared. It was a great location for a new law practice.

During my tenure, Mr. and Mrs. F.O. Mackey were the owners of the hotel. Mrs. Mackey, a former Londoner, was a stickler for propriety. She insisted that gentlemen wear coat and tie in the dining room, where the *pièce de résistance* was buffalo steak. (The Mackeys purchased the buffalo from the Krentz family, whose ranch northeast of Douglas reached its own 100-year anniversary this fall.) The year 2007 marked the 100-year anniversary of the opening of the Gadsden Hotel. To celebrate the centennial, current owners Hartman, Henry, and Robyn Brekhus sponsored a celebration featuring Arizona authors, artists, and musicians. Since I had recently published a book, *Tales of My Southwest*, I was invited to participate.

I am sure the fact that my father and Ezra J. "Bud" Warner had owned the hotel in the 1940s influenced my being asked to attend. Dad had maintained his office in the hotel continually for more than 50 years.

The Gadsden's original wooden frame structure burned on February 7, 1928, and the hotel was rebuilt of solid concrete and reinforced steel. It reopened on May 30, 1929, just before the Great Depression.

When Bud Warner and Dad owned the hotel, they refurbished it by having the ceilings in the lobby gilded with real gold leaf. There are 400 ounces of gold on the ceiling today.

Bud, while on a trip to Acapulco, found a beautiful mosaic ceramic tile inlay, which was installed in the dining room, where it can be observed today. The windows on the mezzanine above the marble staircase leading from the lobby are original Tiffany, made and installed by Tiffany of New York. Today their value is enormous.

Dad and Bud redid the "tap room" and saw to it that the livestock brands of ranchers from southern Arizona and northern Mexico were painted on the walls. Behind the bar and in its center, Bud's and Dad's brands are prominently displayed, along with Granddad's old and famous "Z" brand which he acquired when he bought the San Bernardino Ranch from the John Slaughter family in 1937.

"W" on the jaw and "H" on the hip were the brands from the Las Palomas Ranch, which Dad and four others owned in Chihuahua in the early 1940s. Bud Warner's brands came from his Cienega Ranch ten miles north of Rodeo, New Mexico.

During Pancho Villa's raid on Agua Prieta in 1915, interested observers gathered on the roof of the Gadsden and watched the battle between the revolutionaries and the federal troops across the border.

I know volumes can be written about that grand old hotel where I once maintained my law office. It is good to see the hotel today operating and maintained by the Brekhus family, for it is truly a historical treasure and an asset for the city.

By the way, if you want a buffalo steak today, you have to bring your own buffalo.

FOOL'S GOLD

The water works in Douglas belongs to the city and is operated as a city enterprise, with three water commissioners. The commissioners' duty is to control and manage all matters pertaining to the city's water system.

In the spring of 1968 Jack Davis, a senior engineer at the Phelps Dodge smelter in Douglas; L.R. Acosta, an accountant; and Vic Daniels, owner of Copper Maintenance Company–all City of Douglas water department commissioners–decided it was time to drill a new water well for the city. Once it was determined that a new city well was needed, the commission issued a call for bids for a contract to drill the well. Notice was published in the Douglas newspaper and in trade journals and was posted on all local bulletin boards.

The well was to be drilled next to the city water department offices, then in the 300 block of Eleventh Street, not quite a city block from the Gadsden Hotel.

Once the call for bids had been issued, the next step was to review them. The commissioners met on the date set, examined the bids, and determined that Earl Lohn, a well driller from Willcox, was the lowest qualifying bidder. The contract was awarded to Earl, and he brought his well rig down to Douglas, where he set it up next to the water department building. Earl was a crotchety man about sixty years of age, but he was possessed of a good, dry sense of humor.

Once the rig was set up, drilling commenced, and many residents watched the new show for the first two or three days, after which only a small handful continued to follow the well's progress.

One of the most interested observers was Sam Levy of Douglas, a member of the family that had established Levy Brothers stores, first in Douglas, then in Tucson. Levy's maintained a large store in downtown Tucson on Scott and Pennington for many years until it was moved to the El Con shopping center on East Broadway.

Sam was retired, a man of leisure with little to do except scout around town visiting his many friends.

The drilling project fascinated Sam. He went early each morning, before any of the other observers, to see what progress had been made.

Each day when Earl arrived at the rig to begin the day's drilling, Sam had already made his initial inspection and was full of questions.

"How deep are you? What kind of strata have you encountered? Have you hit hard rock? How many feet do you think you will drill today? When will the well be finished? How much water will it produce? Will the water be sweet and potable?" And a myriad of other questions.

Sam finally got Earl's goat.

One evening after work, when everybody had left the drill site, Earl sprinkled some iron pyrite (fool's gold) granules in the sand left from the discharge from the day's work.

The iron pyrite filings shone with golden brilliance in the sand. Upon Sam's arrival the following morning at the well site, he saw the glistening specks in the sand. He could hardly wait for Earl, to show him his discovery.

When Earl arrived, Sam immediately took him to the place where he had found the gold. "Earl, tell me, what do these shiny specks mean?"

"Well, I'll be damned. We must have struck gold."

Before nightfall, the whole town knew of the city's new gold strike, for Sam had been busy all day telling everybody he ran into about the city's wonderful good fortune.

THE BEEKEEPER

On a beautiful April morning of 2008, I was in my front yard in Tucson enjoying the delicious fragrance of the grapefruit tree in full bloom. I noticed there were no honeybees tending to the pollen and blossoms. The smell was intoxicating, and any bee worth his salt should have been eagerly gathering pollen for his colony.

I recalled reading that the African killer bees had crossbred with the European honeybees, causing some people to believe that this had a very pronounced and significant impact on the current bee population. A few say that the cross of the two produces a new strain that is sterile, but who knows?

I was reminded of the delightful summer in 1944 that I spent at the San Bernardino Ranch fifteen miles east of Douglas with my aunt and uncle, Ella and Morris Browder.

Morris had a good friend, Paul Nickols, an inspector with the immigration and naturalization service in Douglas. Paul and his wife and two sons lived just a couple of blocks away from my grandparents, Marion and Teresa Williams, in Douglas.

When Paul was not working on the line, he was tending his bees. He was registered as a certified beekeeper with the State of Arizona and had a bee stamp which had been granted by the regulatory agency in Phoenix. Paul owned fifty or sixty colonies of honeybees which he placed around Cochise County (with the permission of the landowners, of course). He had twenty-five colonies at the San Bernardino, where mesquite trees grew in great abundance to a height of ten to fifteen feet. In May and June, the mesquite trees produced beautiful long, yellow blossoms which the bees loved. They produced golden honey with a unique and delicious taste.

Paul had given four colonies to Uncle Morris and one colony to me. I was fifteen years old and an eager student of beekeeping. During that summer I learned a great deal about bee husbandry, and from my one colony produced some of the golden honey, as well as a few small, square boxes of sweetly filled honeycomb, which we loved to chew. It was much like chewing gum because of its sweetness and similarity to Wrigley's Juicy Fruit.

I learned that if I wore a pith helmet, covered with beekeeper's mesh fastened properly to the shirt collar, and a khaki-colored long-sleeved shirt and trousers with cuff-keepers, I was almost impervious to bee stings.

Nevertheless, I made sure to approach the hives with caution and with a bellows hand smoker containing gunny sacks drenched in used motor oil which had been fired. I poured smoke into the hive, which quieted the bees as I came near.

The queen bee was of great interest to me. She was much larger than the worker bees. We kept her in the bottom two "supers" (trays) with a separating metal screen which allowed worker bees to freely circulate through the hive but kept the queen in her brood chambers on the first and second stories of her domain. The queen could not lay her eggs above the restraining mesh which separated the upper supers from the lower supers. The baby brood chambers were separated from the upper stories where the workers produced pure honey.

Above the second level, each super contained eight to ten "frames" which held factory-manufactured honeycomb wax foundations. These foundations were held in place with fine copper wires so that the bees could build upon them, making hexagonal chambers to be filled with honey and then capped. The supers were about ten inches in height.

Every now and then, a queen bee would wear out and die or "swarm" away from the colony if it became too large. This required replacement with another queen. We ordered new, healthy young queens from bee supply houses in the Midwest and southern United States. The new young queens arrived by mail in small, wooden blocks into which had been drilled holes. One end was covered with a fine brass mesh. Into the hole would be inserted a queen and three or four worker bees to attend to her needs. In the other end of the wooden block–which was about an inch-and-a-quarter square by three inches long–a piece of peppermint candy was inserted as a stopper. The worker bees ate the peppermint candy and processed it into royal nectar to feed to their queen to keep her healthy while en route to her new home.

Upon arriving at the new home, which was the existing colony, the entire block of wood, peppermint candy and all, was placed in the brood chambers of the colony. Worker bees on the outside, as well as the queen's attendants inside her chambers, ate the peppermint candy, thereby eliminating the peppermint plug. It took some time to eat the stopper, which permitted the old worker bees to become acquainted with their new monarch and accept her. Once acquainted with their new queen, they would not kill her when she emerged from her shipping crate to set about her duties of laying eggs to populate the colony.

If there was an old queen bee in the hive, the new one would seek her out and kill her, thereby becoming the new and sole monarch of the colony.

To make it easy to find the queen when we wanted to find her, we placed a small dot of red fingernail polish on her back.

You might ask, was I ever stung? And of course the answer is "yes." I was stung a number of times by bees that were able to somehow work through the protective clothing I wore. I was also stung in another more unusual fashion. Bees would attach to my clothing from time to time, leaving their stingers in the fabric, usually my trousers.

A bee's stinger has very small barbs which keep it from being easily withdrawn from the host to which it is attached when the bee stings. The bee will fly away, pulling the stinger from its body and leaving it implanted wherever it has stung, in either a person or an object.

Occasionally, when I put on my trousers after tending to my bees, I would inadvertently slap or rub against stingers left in the trousers, and in so doing, inject them into my skin, stinging myself just as the bee might have done. This might be several days after the bee had gifted me with its stinger. The effect of the sting was the same as if it had been freshly planted in my hide, and it still hurt like the devil.

Although not allergic to bee stings, all I could think to do when I was stung was run and holler. When I was stung more than once, all I could do was run faster and farther and holler louder.

You must never remove the stinger by grasping it between the forefinger and thumb, for to do so merely compresses the bulb at the end of the stinger, introducing venom into your body. The proper way to remove a stinger is to take a knife blade or other similar type of sharp-edged object and scrape the stinger from its place of implantment.

I also learned early on that bees tolerate light-colored clothing, such as white or tan khakis, far better than dark clothing, such as Levis. A bee will almost always sting the Levi-wearer before it will sting a person wearing the lighter-colored clothing.

I was once involved in capturing a wild colony of bees that had made their home in the shale rock bank of Silver Creek west of the San Bernardino Ranch headquarters. How did we find that colony? Well, I'll tell you. There were a lot of bees gathered around water at a stock tank where cattle watered, about a quarter-mile from their home. We did not know where the colony was. It took two of us to locate the bees' domicile.

At the tank where they had gathered to drink, we took some flour and sprinkled it on the watering bees. This made them look white, of course.

We watched when they took off to determine their flight path. We would follow the white bees to the point where we lost them. Then more flour would be applied to more bees back at the watering hole, and the lookout, standing at the place where he last saw the white bees and watching carefully, would soon see another white bee flying past him. He would follow that bee to the point where he next lost him and wait until another white bee flew by. Following the course of the flight of the white bees soon led us to the bees' home.

But back to Tucson, my flowering grapefruit tree, and the dearth of honeybees. Why are there no bees? I don't know. Will the scarcity of bees have an effect on the fruit crop for next year? I don't know. I do know, however, that bees are necessary to cross-pollinate for better fruit production.

Where have all the flowers gone? Wherever the bees are.

PRIVATE LIVES

COWBOY GOLFERS

Did you ever see the photograph of two cowboys and their horses on a putting green? The cowboys are golfing, with their golf bags slung over the saddle horns while the horses watch as the putting duel unfolds.

One cowboy-golfer is stroking the ball toward the hole, while the other is cautiously waiting, hoping the ball won't fall. If it does, he loses the match.

The putting cowboy is Gus Wien. Both are dressed in their usual cowboy outfits.

Gus Wien's sister was Beatrice Wien, a teacher in the Douglas public school system. Miss Wien was born in Russellville, Arizona, a mining camp in northwestern Cochise County. In its heyday, Russellville claimed a population of about one hundred souls The town was relocated around the turn of the century to the town of Johnson, also in Cochise County. Johnson owed its existence to the Peabody copper mine. Its post office was dedicated on April 5, 1900, and continued in existence until it was closed on November 29, 1929. At its zenith, Johnson had a community of one thousand. Today it is a ghost town.

Miss Wien taught me sixth grade in 1941 at the grammar school. I was just a boy of twelve, never a dedicated student. Miss Wien was a formidable and fine teacher. When she told the class to do something, we did it. There was no equivocation or retreat from her assignments.

I recall one chore for the class was to learn by rote three verses of the poem

Gus Wien, brother of Beatrice Wien, author's sixth-grade teacher.
Photo courtesy of Arizona Historical Society/Tucson. AHS# 28731

written by Samuel Taylor Coleridge, *The Rime of the Ancient Mariner*. You may recall the words, "water, water everywhere, nor any drop to drink."

Memorizing written material was never my strong suit in school, and I wondered how in the world I would ever learn those verses. They had to be memorized over a weekend. Members of the class were expected to recite the verses without error, a seemingly impossible task for me.

I recall working like a beaver that weekend trying to memorize that darn thing, and I vividly remember being called on in class.

"Benny, please recite for us three verses of *The Rime of the Ancient Mariner*."

I recited with a few errors, not so many as to fail, but at the same time I did not crown myself with glory in my presentation.

In another assignment, the class was told to write a story about a doughnut. We were given a weekend to write it and told to submit it on the following Monday for review and grading. I never got my story back, although I did write it and turn it in as instructed.

I went on with my schooling and eventually attended the University of Arizona, where I earned a law degree. When I finished law school, I took the bar examination and upon passing, returned to Douglas to practice my new profession.

After I was established in my new law practice for some time, I received a telephone call from Miss Wien one day asking for an appointment. I was delighted that my old schoolteacher thought enough of me to seek a professional consultation.

At our conference, I learned that her brother was August ("Gus") Wien of Cochise, Arizona. As mentioned, he is the putter in the photograph which I am recalling in my mind's eye.

Miss Wien had brought with her my story, written on March 24, 1941, as the language assignment which she had given to our 6A class.

"Benny, you might want to keep this story as a memento." I was delighted, and I did keep that story. Recently I ran across my story about the doughnut while reviewing some old records. That story is called "Tommy's Doughnut," and it goes as follows:

"One fine morning in the early fall Tommy woke up and got dressed to go down to breakfast. Just as he was through Uncle John came down to get his breakfast. Now all Tommy had for his breakfast was cereal, bacon, and tea. It with [sp] hot cocoa. But Uncle John had doughnuts and coffee. Tommy liked doughnuts very much. So as soon as Uncle John sat down at the table Tommy went over and looked at the doughnuts with very wide eyes. Uncle John said, 'I know what you are thinking about. You may have one doughnut.' So Tommy was happy the rest of the morning."

Guess I've always liked happy endings.

The photo of Gus Wien and his golfing opponent reposed on the wall along with other cowboy pictures at La Placita restaurant in Tucson for several years. The Mexican restaurant was recently remodeled with a more Asian motif and the photo was given by the new owner to an admirer.

If you should run across a photo of a couple of cowboys, with their mounts standing by and golf bags slung over their saddle horns, the chances are good that the cowboy handling the putter is Gus Wien.

BARE FACTS REVEALED

In the early 1960s, Dale Fenter, a young lawyer who had been practicing with the Gentry, McNulty and Kimble firm in Bisbee, and I became law partners. We set up offices in the professional building across the street from the post office on Tenth Street in Douglas.

Dale was married to Maryanne, a real sweetheart of a gal. They had three children, two boys and a girl.

Dale and I did well enough in the practice to keep the wolf from the door and pay our bills in a prompt manner.

Dale was a cowboy type whose family had been ranching around Greaterville, Arizona, where he grew up. As a young boy, he rode his horse, Prince, from the Fenter ranch to the Greaterville school, where he tied him to the hitching rail in front of the school house. When classes were over at the end of the day, he rode Prince home.

Having grown up around Greaterville on his family's ranch, Dale was never troubled by any of the formalities and niceties of the more sophisticated city lifestyle.

One always knew when Dale came to visit, for he gave a short whistle–which announced his presence–then opened the door and proceeded into the house. He was always upbeat, happy, and a pleasure to be around.

One day the flying bug bit Dale, so he took lessons at Douglas. After completing his lessons, he soloed and was granted a private pilot's license.

In those days, Phelps Dodge Corporation maintained a big business presence in Douglas. As a matter of fact, the western general offices of PD were located there, where most of the corporate business west of New York City was transacted.

A number of geologists and geophysicists lived in Douglas and traveled world-wide, constantly exploring for new mineral deposits. Copper was PD's primary product. Phelps Dodge in those days was the second largest copper company in the United States.

One of PD's senior geophysicists was John Sumner. He resided with his wife, Nancy, and children in Douglas on Ninth Street, where the family maintained a lovely and comfortable home.

John was an experienced pilot. He hangared his plane at the Douglas Municipal Airport, not a mile from his house.

Dale–always enterprising–approached John, and they soon reached an understanding whereby Dale could use the plane when he wanted to. This arrangement brought the two of them into frequent contact. They frequently met to discuss aviation matters and, of course, the airplane.

One bright morning in May, Dale went to John and Nancy's home. He wanted to talk to John about using the plane. As was his fashion, when he reached the kitchen door, he opened it, announced his presence with a little whistle, entered, and found himself in the kitchen with Nancy, who was clothed in nothing more than a bra and a pair of panties. Dale abruptly whirled around and quickly exited without saying a word. He was totally embarrassed.

Several days later, after pondering how to broach the matter with John, the two met, and Dale said, "John, there's something that has been troubling me, and I have to get it off my chest."

"What's that?" said John.

"I have to confess to you that I feel I've been seeing too much of Nancy lately."

Whereupon, John burst out laughing. "Nancy told me about it, and I was waiting to run into you to rub it in. I might suggest that in the future you knock on the door and wait until somebody answers before entering."

HAPPY WILLIAMS

One fine Sunday morning in June of 1971, when our daughter Katie and son Ben were young, they asked if we could go fishing at the San Bernardino Ranch. A four-acre pond at the ranch house is fed by three constantly flowing springs which have been a wonderful water source for centuries, as evidenced by round mortar-like holes made long ago in the volcanic bedrock by Indians. They used the holes to grind flour from mesquite beans and wild grains, which they made into cakes to eat.

The pond was created by a dam made from stone and mortar. Stocked with bluegill, crappy, bass, and catfish, it was a great fishing hole.

When the children and I ventured forth to fish, we first went to Safeway to buy some chicken liver, a fine bait for the catfish. We also took a shovel to dig below the dam for nice, big, juicy angleworms that were always to be found in abundance and which provided a most succulent repast for the fish.

When we arrived at the ranch, after a forty-five minute drive over a dirt road, I parked next to the pond and we unloaded our gear from the car.

Happy, our small dog, came with us. Happy had been so named because of a wonderful disposition, which made her a great pet. She had followed the kids home one day when just a puppy, refused to leave our doorstep, and was raised by us.

I took the shovel and went below the dam, where I dug up a number of beautiful angleworms which we carefully baited on the hooks and cast out into the pond.

The fish weren't biting on worms.

"Well, kids, let's get that liver out and see how it'll work. Maybe the fish would rather have a different diet today."

I cut the liver into small pieces and baited three hooks. We cast them into the pond and got nary a bite.

One of the kids retrieved the bait and left the line on the shore while going off to pursue some beautiful dragonflies. Happy came along the bank, found the liver, and naturally swallowed it–hook, line, and sinker.

Soon Katie ran to me crying, "Daddy, something's wrong with Happy. She seems to be gagging, and fishing line is hanging out of her mouth."

I went to investigate, and sure enough, Happy had swallowed the liver, hook and all, with the line still attached. The line was dangling from the dog's gagging mouth.

"Kids, don't yank on that line. It might set the hook so we can't get it out. I'm afraid to do anything other than go to town and see if we can call Dr. Behney, the vet up in Bisbee. Hold Happy and the line, but don't pull on it. Keep Happy from moving as much as you can."

We quickly packed up our gear, got in the car, and motored back to town, where I called both Dr. Behney's office and his home in Bisbee. I got a recording on both lines telling me that the doctor had gone to Tucson for the weekend and would not be available. Until Monday.

The kids were beside themselves. "Daddy, what are we going to do? Happy's going to die! Please do something."

"Well, kids, the only thing I can think of is to call Dr. Montgomery." He had been our family physician for years–a fine doctor and a great friend.

I finally reached Dr. Montgomery, or Bosco as we called him, at a local hospital where he was chief of the medical staff.

"Bosco, our dog Happy swallowed some liver with a fish hook attached to a fishing line, and we don't know what to do. I tried to get in touch with the vet in Bisbee, but he's away. The kids are frantic and crying buckets."

"Okay, Benny, bring your dog out to the hospital and I'll look at her. You know I'm really not a vet, though."

We took Happy to the hospital and carried her in. Bosco took one look at her. "Let's take her to the X-ray room." He placed her on the X-ray table and took a couple of pictures.

"I can't tell, but it looks like the hook is positioned so it might possibly pass on through if we cut the fishing line at the dog's mouth. Check for the next couple of days and see if the fishhook passes through.

"Benny, you know we're not supposed to take X-rays of animals here in the hospital. This isn't a veterinary facility. I have to make some record, however, so I'm just going to call this patient Happy Williams."

We thanked Bosco profusely and took Happy home, where we watched her for the next few days. Sure enough, as Bosco thought, the fishhook passed through and there were never any other problems for the hospital's new patient, Happy Williams.

AN EVENING OF SHOOTING

In 1972, when my Little Flower (Daisy) and I were living in Douglas, my cousin Tooter and his wife Betty came from Albuquerque to visit. Betty's father had been a big-game hunting guide in Mexico. Betty had grown up around guns and shooting all her life.

As kids, Tooter and I loved guns, and Stoeger's catalog (the shooters' bible) was our constant companion when we were growing up. We could tell you what gun appeared on page 73 and the caliber of the rifle appearing on page 107.

Tooter was a registered gun dealer. He was not so much into the commercial end of gun buying and selling as he was for his own and his family's use. As a dealer, he was permitted to do a lot of shooting at special rates, as well as to buy guns and ammo at reduced prices. Tooter and Betty both enjoyed shotgun shooting, and we thought it might be fun to introduce them to a few of our gun-loving friends.

Little Flower and I had some wonderful neighbors, Dr. Harry Smith and his wife, Jean. They lived only a block from us, and we socialized frequently. We invited them to come for cocktails. Harry, Tooter, and I were going dove hunting the following day, and we wanted to plan the hunt.

While we were enjoying our cocktails, the conversation turned to scatter gun shooting. Jean had recently taken instruction in trap shooting and truly enjoyed it. She had become rather proficient for a novice, and her exuberance for the sport was really showing that evening. The topic of ladies' trapshooting became so intense that it was all Jean could talk about; she was really monopolizing the conversation. With each drink, her shooting prowess improved.

All this time, Betty sat listening quietly to Jean's stories about her fine shooting. Finally, in a short pause in her dissertation, Jean turned to Betty and said, "Have you ever done any shotgun shooting?"

"Yes, I've done some."

"Do you like it?"

"Yes, I do."

"Where did you do your shooting?"

"In and around Albuquerque and other towns in New Mexico."

"Betty, you should try trap shooting. I think you could really become captivated by the sport."

"Maybe so."

"How much shooting have you done, Betty?"

"Well, as a matter of fact, I've done quite a bit. I'm the New Mexico State ladies' champion trap shooter."

Jean's jaw dropped, and not another word was heard. Shortly thereafter, she said, "Harry, I think we'd better go home and check on that pot roast I've got in the oven."

Thus ended an evening of shooting.

A SPOT ON THE RUG

"Have you noticed there's a spot on the rug?" It was the spring of 1997, and Daisy (my Little Flower) and I were talking in the family room.

"Yes. It was probably left by one of the grandkids when they last visited. It looks terrible. What should we do about it?"

"I think we ought to have it cleaned."

"Fine. Let's get somebody to clean it." This was done.

The rug came back in immaculate condition, so much brighter that it looked brand new.

Little Flower said, "You know, that clean rug shows just how dirty our sofa is."

"You're right. What should we do?"

"Well, I think we ought to have it cleaned also."

"Fine, let's do it."

She called the cleaners. They took the sofa to their shop, cleaned it, and returned it looking brand new.

Not long after that, Little Flower said, "You know those two occasional chairs? We've had them an awful long time. They look shabby. I think we should do something about them."

"Okay. What do you think should be done?"

"I think they ought to be recovered."

"I agree. Let's select a fabric and get it done."

We got in touch with the upholstery man. He looked the chairs over. "Yes, they could stand a new upholstery job. Pick out a fabric and I'll do them."

A few weeks later, we were sitting in the family room looking over the new decor. Little Flower said, "You know, the new upholstery and the clean rug make those drapes look awful. I think they should be replaced."

"Well, I guess you're right. Call someone and see about having them replaced. We'll have to pick out a suitable fabric."

A few weeks later the new drapes were installed, and they looked simply wonderful. We were sitting in the family room enjoying the new atmosphere when Little Flower said, "Those valances above the new drapes have been there an awfully long time. They're really out of style."

"Well, I guess so. What should we do about them?"

"We ought to have them replaced."

"Okay. I'll see who can make new ones."

After contacting some people who did that kind of work, we selected new fabric to cover the valances. They were built according to our specifications and installed. They looked splendid.

Of course, to go with our new decor, the room had to be repainted.

Sitting in the family room not long afterward, I said, "You know, Little Flower, this room really looks great now."

"You're right."

"Do you have any idea what it cost to do this?"

"No."

"Well, first of all the rug, then the sofa, then the two occasional chairs, then the drapes, then the valances, then the paint job. Do you realize that the whole thing came to $8,695.40?"

"Really? But don't you think it's worth it?"

"Of course. Absolutely."

Men, beware of a spot on the rug!

BABYSITTERS EXTRAORDINAIRE

In March of 2002, my wife, Daisy, and I were asked to babysit our grandchildren, Natalie and Pierce Braun, ages seven and two-and-a-half. I call Daisy "Little Flower" because she is small (5 feet, 3 inches) and named for a flower.

Natalie is a very bright child, most precocious and enterprising. Her younger brother, Pierce, is large for his age (off the charts), and is inquisitive and into everything. We were to take care of them for three whole days and nights. We were ecstatic with joy, never having been permitted to do this before. I even went so far as to prepare a legal document for their parents, Todd and Kate, to sign, authorizing Little Flower and me to be the temporary guardians, should legal matters require. Armed with this power of attorney, we could authorize medical and hospital care, although we weren't expecting any problems.

Little Flower and I arrived at the Brauns' in Phoenix on a Friday evening, unpacked our bags, and eagerly undertook our assignment. Supper at Garcia's Mexican Restaurant on Camelback is a Friday-night family tradition. Our oldest granddaughter, Beth, age twenty-one, had graciously offered to care for Pierce while the rest of us went to dinner. Todd told us to use their Mercedes while they were gone since Pierce's baby seat was already installed in the car and we would not have to fool around changing it to our own.

When Little Flower, Natalie, and I arrived at Garcia's, I misjudged the distance to the parking bumper, mashing the weed guard up under the front end of the Mercedes with a loud scraping sound. I got out, surveyed the damage and announced to the others that it wasn't bad. We then proudly marched into Garcia's to join the rest of the family.

After supper, we returned to Todd and Kate's, played games, and told bedtime stories well past the night curfew, then put the kids to bed. Little Flower agreed to get up with Pierce the first night. He usually had to have a feeding and a wet-diaper change. The second night I was to get up with Pierce.

Our other son-in-law, Jim Boyd, had invited me to play golf with him the next day. Jim dropped me off at the Brauns about five in the evening after a thoroughly enjoyable game. The door was locked, so I rang the bell. Natalie and Little Flower opened it. Both were excited and flustered. Little Flower's voice was urgent: "Ben, we've got a problem!"

Then Natalie blurted out, "Grampsy, Grampsy, Pierce's been eating poison!"

Completely stunned, I exclaimed, "What happened? Tell me!"

"He got into a tube in the bathroom and was brushing his teeth with it," was Little Flower's panicky explanation.

I said, "Nat, please bring me the tube, quickly." Then I asked Little Flower, "What happened? What's going on?"

"While Natalie and I were making popcorn, Pierce brushed his teeth with this!" She handed me the tube Natalie had brought. It was labeled Lotrimin (a cure for athlete's foot). "For external use only. Keep out of reach of children. If swallowed, get medical help or contact a poison control center right away."

We were flustered and not quite sure what to do until Natalie said, "Grampsy, call 911."

I called 911 and said, "My name is Ben Williams and my grandson, two-and-a-half years old, has brushed his teeth with Lotrimin."

They said, "We can't handle that. We'll connect you with the Fire Department."

This was the Phoenix Fire Department–I don't know which substation–but once connected, I repeated, "My name is Ben Williams and my grandson has been brushing his teeth with Lotrimin."

"You need Poison Control, not the Fire Department."

"Please connect me with Poison Control."

"Sure. Just a moment."

They connected me. I was told it was the Poison Control Center at the University of Arizona in Tucson. Again I identified myself and told them the problem.

In the meantime, Natalie announced, "Grampsy, Kit is leaking water all up and down the hall."

I said, "We'll take care of that in a few moments, Natalie. Let's take care of Pierce first."

Poison Control asked, "How much has the child consumed?" "I don't know, but the tube seems to be about one-third to one-half gone, and there is a notation on the tube that says 'If ingested, get medical help or contact Poison Control.'"

"Has the child been vomiting or showing any unusual symptoms?"

"No, he seems to be okay." I did notice, however, that Pierce was scared to death because all the excitement was focused on him.

Poison Control came back on the phone. "Mr. Williams, keep on eye on the child. He should be all right. We do have a suggestion, however."

"What's that?"

"Next time, use Colgate. It's much better for you."

With Pierce's problem taken care of, we addressed the second crisis.

The Brauns' dog is named Kit. She's a fine-blooded animal, a Pembroke Welch Corgi, grossly overweight. Kit will eat anything that doesn't eat her first. She has legs about six inches long and because of her obesity her belly almost drags the floor when she walks. At the time, she had diabetes, but they didn't know it.

In all the excitement, the big bowl of popcorn made by Little Flower and Natalie had been left on the coffee table in the playroom. Natalie issued another proclamation. "Grampsy, all of the popcorn's gone."

"Great Scott, you don't suppose Kit ate the whole bowl, do you?"

"It's all gone, Grampsy. I'll bet she did."

Little Flower said, "It was a great big bowl."

We looked for Kit and found her in a dark corner under a table in the kitchen. She was stretched out on all fours, looking like she was dying.

"Grampsy, Kit drank all her water. The big bowl's empty."

"She must be thirsty. Give her some more."

We filled it again and set it in front of her. Kit drank it at once.

I asked Natalie, "Does Kit have a vet?"

"Grampsy, I think Mother and Dad left the vet's telephone number with Uncle Benjie."

"Gee, that's great." I called Benjie and described our problem. I said, "The dog has eaten a huge bowl of popcorn. I think she's dying."

Benjie was helpful. "Let me call Dr. Bracken, Kit's vet, and see what he says. I'll call you back when I learn something."

We proceeded to do what we could for the poor dog, which was very little except to offer more water.

A few minutes later, Benjie called back. "The vet says not to give the dog anything more to eat or drink. He also said to watch her overnight and if she's not better in the morning, to give him a call."

"Great Scott, the dog's been drinking copious amounts of water and looks like she's going to explode."

"Well, don't let her have anything more."

About this time, Natalie said, "Grampsy, there's another stream of water down the other hall."

I went to look, and sure enough, there was a big trail, obviously Kit's urine.

"The vet told us to watch Kit overnight, and if she's not better in the morning, to give him a call."

Finally, Little Flower and I put the children to bed. I have never had a problem falling asleep, and this was no exception.

When I awoke in the morning, Little Flower was feeding Pierce his breakfast. She said, "I was up part of the night with Pierce, to change diapers and give him a drink of water. Why don't you look after him now, and I will go back to sleep."

I said, "Okay."

Things proceeded well. We had everything under control.

Todd and Kate called during the day and inquired, "How are things going? Are the kids much trouble?"

Little Flower said, "They are just fine. The kids are just angelic, and we're having a ball. Please enjoy yourselves and don't worry."

That evening, we fed the children and put them down–late as usual, because they wanted to stay up past their usual bedtime.

This was my night at the helm. About 1:30 or 2:00 I was awakened by a cooing sound. It was Pierce, calling quietly from his bed.

I said, "Okay, young man, it's time to change your diaper."

There wasn't any place to change his diaper, so I put him on the rug on the floor. I hadn't changed diapers for many years and always hated handling bowel movements. Without thinking, I lifted Pierce up and whipped out his diaper, only to find a huge BM. There I was, hanging on to him by his two feet, with him lying on his back and his bottom all smeared with goo. I couldn't put him down or lift him up. No clean diapers or anything else was within reach. I was in a terrible spot, gagging from the smell, hardly able to catch my breath.

Pierce announced with an impish smile, "Grampsy, poo-poo."

"Yes, dear boy, I just discovered that."

Finally I decided the thing to do was to lift him by his hands and feet, somehow get a diaper on the rug, put him on top of that, then clean him up and change the diaper. The clean diapers were on the dresser on the other side of the room. I lifted Pierce with both hands, went to the dresser, picked up a fresh diaper in my teeth and dropped it on the carpet. Then I put Pierce on the diaper and cleaned him. Necessity is the mother of invention.

Of course, by this time Pierce was wide awake and not particularly interested in going back to sleep. I must say, I wasn't either. I sang quietly to Pierce so as not to wake Little Flower. After a while we both got sleepy, so I put him back in bed and said, "Here you go. Back to sleep now, and we'll get up and have breakfast in the morning." He did go to sleep, finally. We woke early in the morning and were having breakfast when Little Flower came into the kitchen. "How did things go last night?"

"Just super!"

We fed Pierce and took care of both kids during that day and night as well. We called Todd and Kate to report that everything was under control and we were having a ball.

In the meantime, and unknown to us, Natalie had called her parents and reported, "Grampsy wrecked the Mercedes; Pierce has been eating poison and we had to call Poison Control; Kit nearly died and we had to call the vet."

We didn't learn of this telephone call until much later, after Todd and Kate returned from San Francisco.

When they arrived, they asked, "How was it?"

"Wonderful," we said. "Everything went well. We had a marvelous time with the children, enjoyed every minute of it–and we want to take care of them again soon."

A couple of days later, Todd mentioned to me casually, "You know, we have such a wonderful time being with our children that we're going to take them with us from now on. We really like to have them close to us. We'll send Kit to the doggy hotel. "

I said nothing.

I wonder why we've not been invited back to babysit?

BREAKFAST ON THE TERRACE

I awoke at my usual hour of 5:00 a.m. on Friday, July 15, 2005, and went to the kitchen to make my coffee. I looked out the window and there was a bobcat, an animal affectionately known to U of A fans as a "wildcat." He was sitting on his haunches in a nice, cool, grassy spot on my lawn overlooking the city. I live in the foothills where the city view is quite beautiful.

Mr. Wildcat was dining on a juicy, freshly killed cottontail rabbit. He was thoroughly enjoying his breakfast and little could divert his attention.

I got my camera. Bob was only twenty feet away, but the light was really not good enough for any worthwhile photos. I snapped a couple of shots and the flash distracted him enough from his meal that he looked up at me. I could almost hear him say, "Hey, Bud, don't bother me, I'm eating breakfast."

"Don't call me Bud," I said. "If you must call me anything, let it be Ben."

"Okay, Ben, but move on. Can't a cat have a little privacy so he can enjoy breakfast?"

"You have invaded my territory and you have no business here on my lawn," I replied.

"I have just as much business here as you do, Ben. I'm sure you don't want to get into a discussion of whose rights are prior, animal rights or human rights. Who was on this earth first?"

"Bob," I said, beginning to get angry, "you are eating my bunny."

Bob lounging in author's yard after breakfast

"Listen," he said, "who came to these grounds first, you the human race or us animals? As far as I am concerned, this is free game. Have you forgotten the old legal premise that the hunter who first reduces game to his possession is the legal owner thereof?"

With that statement, he got up, walked around the lawn and burped a couple of times.

I couldn't argue with Bob on this point because the old English common law says that is precisely correct.

Feeling exasperation at having been bested by a damn bobcat, I retreated to the kitchen and made my coffee. On returning, I saw that Bob had returned to his breakfast and was happily relishing every morsel.

"You know it's been two or three days since I've had a good meal, and I'd rather you didn't bother me," Bob said. "Ben, why don't you buzz off?"

I noticed he was eating bones and all. "From everything I hear, roughage is good for one's heart and lowers the cholesterol level," he said.

Then he muttered, "You get out of here and I will soon be on my way."

I went to take my shower, and on returning for my coffee, I saw Bob leaving. He went over the wall, and nary a bit of his breakfast remained on the terrace except for the little cotton-like powder puff of a tail from which the bunny gets its name.

As he left, he said, "So long, Ben. I have to go now and find a cool shady spot where I can lie around all day. You know, these hot Tucson days are beastly. They are so hot they can burn the warts off the devil. You know this terrible heat is not good for the digestion. I'm going to find a cool, shady tree. See you, Ben."

"Go to the devil," I said, "and please don't return."

SOUTH OF
GRINGOLAND

A ROSE BY ANY OTHER NAME . . .

Just beyond the canyon into which the Nacozari River meandered, there used to be a colony on the road to Moctezuma called Pozo Hediondo. Not much more than a wide spot in the road, it had a population at that time of about fifty people–men, women, boys, and girls.

The translation from Spanish to English of "Pozo Hediondo," according to *Velasquez Revised Spanish-English Dictionary*, is "stinky well." It was so named because of the foul smell caused by minerals in the water well. The natives had become accustomed to the smell and taste of the water, so it no longer bothered them.

After being asked for so many years where they were from, the fair maidens of Pozo Hediondo became tired of the implications arising from the name of their hometown. Finally, in desperation, they banded together and sent an emissary to the governor of Sonora at his official office in Hermosillo.

The emissary carried a petition signed by all the ladies. It stated that after years of insults arising from the name of their town, it was felt proper that a name change from "Pozo Hediondo" to "Bella Esperanza" (Beautiful Hope) was appropriate.

After due consideration, the governor agreed that the petition was well taken, and by official act declared the name of the town to be changed to Bella Esperanza.

Now, when asked where they are from, the young maidens gleefully respond,

"We're from Beautiful Hope, Sonora."

If you search, you may be lucky enough to find a new map with the official name, "Bella Esperanza," clearly printed thereon.

SAN NICOLÁS

In 1940, when I was eleven years old, Dad and two of my uncles, Morris Browder and Frank Barcelo, had a little mining prospect going in northern Sonora eighty-five miles south of Douglas. They called it "La Colorada." The road to the property was narrow and winding, and from its location at the top of the mountain you could see switchbacks on six different levels. It was remote and high in the rugged mountains of Sonora.

Dad and his partners had been working there for six or eight months and had sent ore samples to Douglas for assay. The results were disappointing. Dad was going back down to the property to recommend that the project be scrapped. He asked if I would like to go along.

"We'll leave at first light and return tomorrow night. It'll be a long day."

"I'll be ready, Dad," I eagerly replied.

We left as planned and arrived at the property after a hard morning's drive, where Dad delivered the bad news.

"We can't make any money on this mine, so let's close her down," he announced after sharing the assays with Morris and Frank.

Everyone got busy packing up gear and breaking camp. A Mexican worker had a mangy old dog in the camp named "San Nicolás" (St. Nicholas). He was all skin and bones, as pickings and scraps were slim. Juan asked us to take his dog to Moctezuma, thirty miles away.

"Okay, put him in Frank's car."

Uncle Frank had a small, two-door Chevrolet coupe with no back seat. I asked if I could ride back with Morris and Frank and San Nicolás. They were great fun to be with.

The bean pot, which had been on the campfire for a couple of days, was still half full when it was dumped on the ground. San Nicolás immediately seized upon the opportunity and ate every bean without so much as chewing a single one.

On the way to Moctezuma with San Nicolás, Frank said he wanted to stop at a little ranch to pick up some mescal. He always enjoyed a good drink, so we stopped at a little *ranchito* where he bought two five-gallon cans of homemade mescal. He put them in the back of the car with the dog and me. Each can was stoppered with a little wooden plug which had been wrapped in a small piece of cloth to keep the mescal from sloshing out. Nevertheless, a lot of the potent liquor leaked from the cans, creating a intoxicating smell in the small compartment.

Remember, there was no back seat in Frank's car, just the two mescal cans, San Nicolás, the mining equipment, and me. After picking up the mescal, we jostled along for ten or fifteen kilometers, when all of a sudden San Nicolás got sick, no doubt from the mescal fumes, the undigested beans, and the jolting ride. Suddenly there were beans all over the back of the car and me. San Nicolás had puked all over me, my shirt, pants, and shoes. The smell would gag a buzzard. What a mess!

After what seemed to me a never-ending ride, we finally arrived at Juan's house in Moctezuma, where I found a water hose and washed up as best I could.

Every time I see a mangy old dog, I think of my traveling companion, San Nicolás, of many years ago, and I keep my distance.

A "FIVE-STAR" ADVENTURE

In 1952, I was home on leave from active duty, newly assigned to the 822nd Heavy Tank Battalion at Camp Polk, Louisiana. A new second lieutenant leading the second platoon of Charlie Company, I had just completed the company grade officers' armored school course at Fort Knox, Kentucky. After my leave, I was to join my battalion at Camp Irwin, California, where it had been sent for desert training.

While having lunch one day at the Gadsden Hotel with Dad and Shelley Richey, Shelley said, "Benny, I'm going to my ranch down near Bacadéhuachi. Do you want to come along and interpret for me?"

"You bet. When do we leave?"

"Day after tomorrow. We'll go down in my English Land Rover. I can't get away until late in the afternoon, so we'll spend the night in Bavispe. There's a hotel there, and we can go on to the ranch the next morning after breakfast."

I returned to my parents' home, where Daisy and I were staying, and informed Daisy that I would be gone for a couple of days and nights with Shelley. He wanted to talk to his foreman and also look over the steers he was running on the ranch which he had leased near Bacadéhuachi.

The next day, I met Shelley at his office in the Gadsden at 3:00 o'clock in the afternoon. We got in his vehicle and went to the immigration-customs house in Agua Prieta where we obtained crossing documents before proceeding down through

Colonia Morelos, a settlement that Brigham Young was responsible for founding in 1899. Brick houses built by these Mormon settlers can still be seen today.

We arrived in Bavispe after dark. Shelley said, "I know the hotel owner. I'll go get us some accommodations."

On the road to Shelley's ranch

When he returned, I asked, "Did you get a key?"

"No, we don't need one. I'll show you where we're staying."

He took me to a large room where four other men were sleeping on canvas cots in a dormitory-like room. They were all snoring.

Shelley said, "You take a cot, and I'll take one."

"Is this the hotel?"

"Yes," he said.

"I'm sure glad we got a hotel. I would surely have been disappointed if we hadn't been able to get a room at the inn!"

"Well, I've stayed here before, and it's all right. Go ahead and get a good night's rest. See you in the morning."

We got up early the next morning (after a rather iffy "night's rest"), and went to the kitchen in a building next door, where we had a breakfast of chorizo, eggs, tortillas, and *frijoles*, along with some very strong Mexican Café Combaté. A spoon could stand on end in the coffee, it was that strong.

After breakfast we motored along the Bavispe River through some beautiful country. The road was dirt, of course, and difficult to travel, but passable. The rains had come and road repairs hadn't yet been made.

We started to climb into mountains covered with pine trees. After passing through Huachinera, it became obvious that there had been a considerable amount of timbering. Shelley told me there was a nearby sawmill where rough-cut lumber was hewn for shipment to Agua Prieta and the United States.

On reaching the ranch outside of Bacadéhuachi, Shelley announced, "They call the place Rancho Cienegita." It had taken us about three-quarters of an hour over the bumpy and rough track into the high country to reach the Cienegita.

It was a small, typical Mexican ranch with two adobe buildings, each covered with a corrugated iron roof. Pointing to one of the buildings, Shelley said, "That's my place. Take your bag over there. There are two beds. You take the one next to the window, and I'll take the other one.

"I've got to go see Cayetano, my foreman. His wife is a good cook, and she'll fix our meals. We'll eat at Cayetano's house. He'll get us some horses and take us tomorrow morning up to the watering place where I want to look over the steers. We can come back about noon and then head on home once I'm finished."

That evening, Cayetano's wife, Maria, laid out dinner for us in the outdoor kitchen on a wooden table with an oilcloth covering. There was an old number two tomato can in the center of the table which contained knives, forks, and spoons standing on end. Plates had been placed on the table. There was a pot of stew made from venison jerky, potatoes, onions, and green chilies. There were also fresh tortillas and a bowl of *frijoles*. No Mexican meal is complete without *frijoles*.

I put a generous helping of the stew on my plate, along with beans and a tortilla, and began to eat. I must tell you that stew was so damn hot it could have jumped out of the pot right onto my plate.

After dinner, Maria took the enamel-covered plates, wiped them off with a cloth, and stacked them in the corner of her kitchen. She then took the dirty knives, forks, and spoons, wiped them off with the same cloth and stood them back on their ends in the tomato can in the center of the table. I saw this, but said nothing. Shelley looked the other way so that we would not have eye contact.

The next morning at breakfast, I said, "Shelley, I don't think I'm hungry this morning. I'll just have a cup of coffee and a piece of bread."

I had brought with me in my grip two small cans of peaches and one Butterfingers candy bar. Back in our room, I opened one of the cans so that Shelley wouldn't see me, and ate the peaches for my breakfast. I don't remember Shelley having more than a cup of coffee for his breakfast.

After we had eaten, Cayetano brought us horses. We rode up one of the canyons until we arrived at a place where there was a broken-down old windmill and water tank with about twenty-five head of cattle watering and lounging around.

Shelley looked the steers over, and after a bit said, "Well, let's go on back. I've seen enough. They all look pretty good to me."

We rode back to the ranch house where Maria had prepared lunch for us. Lunch consisted of the remainder of the stew from the previous evening, along with *frijoles* and tortillas. I said, "Shelley, I don't think I'm hungry. Thanks, I'll just go lie down for a little bit and wait 'til you're ready to go back."

Once I got to my room, I opened the remaining can of peaches and gobbled them down. It wasn't very long before Shelley came in. "Okay, let's load up and take off."

We got in the Land Rover and proceeded back through Bavispe. I was keeping my eyes open for a restaurant but saw none. The fare at the place we had eaten two mornings before was so bad I didn't want to repeat it.

We arrived at Colonia Morelos about 2:30 in the afternoon. It was hot, and we were tired. And I was famished. "Shelley, do you think we can find a place to get something to eat? I'm absolutely starved."

We asked a man on the street where we could find a restaurant. Pointing, he said, "Mrs. Dominguez over there serves meals."

We went there and entered, to find a middle-aged lady in a room with a wood stove and one wooden table, again with an oilcloth covering. There were no plates or utensils on the table. The floor in the room was dirt. There were chickens running around in and out an open door. Flies were all over the place.

I asked Mrs. Dominguez if she had some food, and she said, "Yes, I've got a pot of chili on the stove and some *frijoles*."

"Please bring the pot and the beans, and by the way, do you have any tortillas?"

She said, "Yes, I made some this morning."

"Bring 'em all."

She brought both pots, the chili and the beans, along with all the tortillas. Shelley and I attacked that food, eating every morsel.

I asked Mrs. Dominguez if she could get a dishcloth to wave over us to keep the flies off Shelley and me while we ate. She obliged; I don't recall swallowing any flies, but there were several near misses.

After that delicious repast, Shelley and I climbed back in the vehicle and motored back to Douglas. It was truly an eventful, interesting, and fun trip–a real Duncan Hines "five-star" experience!

KILOMETER 47
or
A CASE OF FOOT-IN-THE-MOUTH

One late afternoon after work in 1966, four of us "gringos" from Douglas left to go to Nacozari, Sonora, for a weekend of fishing.

We all loaded into my Jeep Wagoneer–Bill Gregory (who owned Gregory Florists, a flower shop-nursery), Aaron Loney (the publisher of the *Douglas Daily Dispatch*), and Sid Moeur (the owner of the Hartford Insurance Agency). We all had obtained our immigration visas at the Mexican consulate in Douglas before leaving.

As we crossed the border at Agua Prieta, I secured a car permit from Mexican customs and we had our tourist visas stamped, legally admitting us into Mexico.

We proceeded toward Nacozari in a very jovial mood, loaded with gear and looking forward with great anticipation to a fun weekend of fishing and frolicking.

I had made arrangements to use my father's staff house at Nacozari, which he leased from the Moctezuma Copper Company, a Mexican subsidiary of Phelps Dodge Corporation. The house had cooking and sleeping facilities.

When we reached kilometer 47 on the dirt road, twenty-one miles south of the border, there was a mud shack with signs out in front which read *"Obligatorio - Alto"* (Obligatory - Stop) and then under that *"Aduana"* (Customs).

As ordered by the signs, I stopped the Jeep and waited patiently in front of the

157

door of the adobe hut. After a few minutes, an unkempt Mexican customs officer came out with his tie loosened and hair disheveled. He had obviously been taking a siesta. It was about 6:00 in the evening.

He came to the driver's side of the car and said in Spanish, *"Donde van?"* (Where are you going?)

I said, "We are going to Nacozari." (*Nos vamos a Nacozari.*)

He then said, *"Aver su permiso para el carro."* (Let me see your car permit.)

I handed him the permit; he examined it most carefully. He was obviously in a very bad mood, probably because we had disturbed his siesta. He then said, *"Donde están sus permisos de imigracion?"* (Where are your immigration visas?)

I turned to my colleagues and said, "He wants to see our immigration visas. Let me have them."

They handed their visas to me and I passed them to the officer. He examined them carefully before returning them, then proceeded to walk slowly around our vehicle. He came back to the driver's side, pointed through the window behind me and said, *"Que son esas cosas?"* (What are those things?)

I told him, *"Son cañas para pescar."* (They are fishing rods.)

"Let me see your fishing licenses."

"We don't have any fishing licenses."

I was very surprised and startled, because he was a customs officer who had nothing to do with enforcement of fishing regulations. He was obviously looking for a *mordida*. He said, "You must have fishing licenses."

I said, *"Es muy tarde para obtenerlos."* (It's very late to get them.)

He said, *"Deben regresar a Agua Prieta para obtener licencias de pescar."* (You have to go back to Agua Prieta to get fishing licenses.)

I was becoming very upset, and I turned to my colleagues and said to them in English, "This sonuvabitch is going to make us go back to Agua Prieta to get fishing licenses!"

At this, the Mexican officer quickly uttered in the king's perfect English, "Sir, I resent being called a son-of-a-bitch!"

I was completely floored! "Officer, where did you learn to speak English like that?"

"I was an exchange officer from the Mexican government to the United States

Military Academy at West Point."

"You must have done something very bad to be posted here at kilometer 47."

He ignored my remark, and then I said to him, "There is a federal tax office in Nacozari, and we will get fishing licenses there."

He said, "If you return this way and you have fish, you are in big trouble if you don't have licenses."

We proceeded to Nacozari, where we had a wonderful weekend, ate many steaks, drank many highballs, and caught many fish.

On our return through kilometer 47 we were most apprehensive, but vastly relieved, to find that our West Pointer was not on duty.

BORDER PATROL

Mary Kidder Rak's book, *Border Patrol*, written in 1938, brought back many memories of people and places well known to me.

She writes about a dry wash through which Mexicans crossed into the United States with ease. When I was mayor of Douglas (1980 to 1988), this "freeway" for Mexican immigration continued not only for illegals but for livestock as well. One of the problems that constantly plagued me as mayor was foraging horses, mules, and jackasses eating greenery in the Douglas City Cemetery. The animals followed the illegals through the ditch and eventually broke into the cemetery, attractive to them because of its lush green grass and shrubbery. The problem got so bad that articles appeared in a small newspaper published by dissidents who wanted to discredit the mayor, council, and city administration.

They griped about livestock trodding the grave sites, and they did have a case because the minute city employees ran off or captured the animals and patched the fence, another group of animals found their way into the cemetery.

Mary Rak's description of the border crossing (known as the "white gate") east of the San Bernardino Ranch is very accurate. My grandfather, Marion L. Williams, owned the San Bernardino Ranch during the late part of the 1930s, all of the 1940s, and part of the 1950s. I have crossed through the white gate into Mexico many times.

The book *Border Patrol* is a compilation of interesting short stories describing incidents involving law enforcement and border patrol officers during the 1940s and 1950s.

Mary writes of John Darling, an immigration inspector stationed at Douglas. I was a boy growing up in Douglas when Dad bought from John and gave to me a homemade motor scooter. I was a sophomore in Douglas High School at the time. Darling was the uncle of Liz Ames who later became a long-term mayor of Douglas in the late 1980s and 1990s.

Mary writes also of Tom Ferrel, who retired from the Border Patrol in Douglas and in 1948 was hired by my father, Ben Williams, to manage his Las Palmas Ranch in Chihuahua. It was a large ranch, 286,000 acres. Tom and I spent a lot of time together during that summer, and I thought the world of him. He gave me his .38 revolver, which he had carried while in the immigration service. I was thrilled with the pistol and told Dad about it. He made me return it, saying it was one of Tom's most treasured possessions.

Sam Westbrook, who is mentioned in the book as well, was an immigration inspector at the Douglas port of entry. He lived on Ninth Street across from the Tenth Street Park, close to my home. I was in his home constantly and played with his son, Richie, who was my age. My cousin, Tooter, was also a good friend of Richie's. The three of us spent a great deal of time together. As a young adult in my early to mid-20s, when I crossed from Agua Prieta to Douglas through the port of entry, frequently Mr. Westbrook would be on duty.

Although he knew Tooter and me very well, Mr. Westbrook always asked our nationality. Why, I'll never know. On one occasion, when asked the question, Tooter responded, "I'm a North American Chinaman."

This infuriated Mr. Westbrook, who said, "You don't have to be smart, and one more remark like that, and I'll jerk you out of that car and take you into the office."

Tooter of course shut up, and we never learned why Westbrook always asked our nationality. He knew my entire family well, for they had all lived in Douglas for many years.

When reading Mary's book, I was taken with the idea that my writing style seems similar to hers. Perhaps that's another reason I enjoyed her book so much.

For anybody who is interested in the Border Patrol and southeastern Arizona as they were in the 30s and 40s, I most heartily recommend *Border Patrol* for a good, easy read.

THE TUNNEL

Douglas had been home to me all my life. When I was growing up, nobody ever thought or heard of narcotic drugs. Alcohol was the drug of choice, marijuana seldom if ever used or even mentioned. So it was a great surprise to me when the discovery of a drug tunnel in Douglas made international news on May 18, 1990.

The press was full of the story–radio, TV, and newspapers. The north end of the tunnel surfaced in a newly built warehouse in Douglas and the south entrance came up in an expensive new home in Agua Prieta, just across the international border. The home and warehouse were built by Francisco Rafael Camarena-Macias. The warehouse was part of a business complex put together by Camarena. It was used in conjunction with a building supply business, which included a cement plant and lumberyard.

Prior to the discovery, Camarena had cut a wide swath in social circles in Douglas and Agua Prieta. I had seen him at the Douglas Golf Club on occasion and had heard many stories of his great wealth and business acumen. Later I learned where that wealth came from. Camarena mysteriously disappeared from the Douglas social and business scene almost immediately before federal officers came down from Phoenix to arrest those involved in the tunnel operation. Unfortunately, the authorities were late; everybody had fled the scene.

Camarena came back into public scrutiny when he was arrested in 1995 off the coast of Mazatlan by Mexican authorities for importation of 6,000 pounds of cocaine. He was tried, found guilty, and sentenced to prison by a Mexican court. For a long time his true identity was not discovered, until sometime around 2001 when somebody tipped the authorities to the fact that it was actually Camarena, the much-wanted felon, who was in the Mexican jail. When this became known, Mexican authorities permitted his extradition to the United States, where it is believed he is presently incarcerated in a place not known to the general public. It is also believed he is serving a long prison term.

Around the time of the tunnel's discovery, I was talking with a law client who was in government service. The topic of the tunnel came up and the officer said, "Oh, yes, we made a film about it. Would you like to see it?"

"Absolutely."

"It's not available for public viewing, but I'll lend it to you overnight, if you won't say where you got it and provided you get it back to me tomorrow."

"Great. I'll take it home and show it to my family."

We viewed the film that night and found it fascinating. I had made an appointment to return the film the following day and also made arrangements for my wife and daughter to go to the warehouse with me to see the tunnel.

We met the officer, who took us to the new warehouse building on First Street in Douglas immediately adjacent to the international boundary fence, just a rifle shot's distance from the Douglas customs house. The warehouse had been secured by local police and U.S. authorities, so we had to be let in by the officer.

As we entered the building I said, "This is nothing but a bare warehouse."

"Do you see that wash rack and drain over there?"

"Yes, I do. It's just a metal grate over a wash drain."

"Come over here and look at it more closely."

We did so, and indeed it was a drain-like grate that had been built into a false door in the floor. Under the false grate was a steel door which, when lifted, revealed a rectangular antechamber four by six feet, with a shaft three feet by three feet wide and forty feet deep. On one side of the shaft was a ladder for a person to climb down into the tunnel. There was a windlass to raise and lower cargo from the surface to the tunnel below. Our daughter, Liz, climbed down the ladder with the officer and entered the tunnel to have a good look.

The tunnel was constructed with a cement roof five feet above floor level. It had electric lights on the ceiling above a cement floor. Also built in was an air-conditioning system, and pockets or spaces in the sides of the tunnel's passageway for storage purposes along its length. It was truly "built to code and specifications." It was quite obvious that an architect had designed the tunnel.

The film we had viewed during the previous evening revealed that on the Mexican side of the border fence was a newly constructed home–Camarena's. In the game room of the home was a pool table. The pool table rested on a false floor that raised three feet when a hydraulic lift was activated. Under this was an antechamber approximately six by eight feet. The chamber had electric lights and a windlass and ladder down to the bottom of the shaft, similar to ones in Douglas.

The film showed a sprinkler head in the lawn outside the home that, when turned, elevated the false floor and pool table in the game room.

I asked how the builders disposed of the earth from the shaft and tunnel without being discovered. I was told that a new bridge was being built by the city of Agua Prieta south of town, and that is where the earth was dumped at night so as not to attract attention. The local populace thought it was just part of the road construction for the bridge parapet.

Later I ran into a friend who was a lieutenant in the Douglas police department and asked him how in the world they had discovered the tunnel. He told me there had been rumors for some time of the existence of a tunnel in Douglas and Agua Prieta, but that the authorities had not been able to locate it. He also said that the comings and goings of the semitrailer used to transport lumber to Douglas from Tucson and Phoenix had been under surveillance for some time. A truck with its bed loaded with cocaine had been interdicted around Chandler, Arizona, and the driver arrested.

Once arrested, and with adequate pressure from the officers, the driver began to "sing like a bird." He told the officers about the location of the tunnel in the Camarena home in Agua Prieta. Armed with that information, United States and Mexican authorities gathered one night at the Camarena home to find the tunnel. They looked for some time before finding the entrance. As a matter of fact, they had sent for a jackhammer and were about to drill through the concrete in the floor of the house to find it, but just before they started to do the jackhammering, an officer turned a water sprinkler head on the front lawn of the home and the hydraulic lift in the playroom of the house was activated, lifting the pool table to reveal the tunnel's Mexican entrance.

The street value of the cocaine seized at Chandler was estimated to be $21 million. There had been considerable speculation as to the high cost of the construction of the

Author emerging from tunnel in the building materials warehouse, on the U.S. side

tunnel, but when compared to the value of the confiscated cocaine and when considering the amount and value of the cocaine that had previously been smuggled through the tunnel, the construction cost was nominal.

What happened to the tunnel? The Mexicans stated they had poured concrete into the opening on their side and sealed it. The American authorities continued to show the tunnel on the U.S. side to government people, including elected officials and law enforcement personnel. After the property was discovered in Douglas, it was seized and forfeited to the government.

The tunnel at Douglas was one of the most sophisticated of the many tunnels that have been discovered along the United States-Mexico border, including those at Nogales, Mexicali, and San Diego, also in Texas.

One might ask: When will tunnels cease to be constructed? The answer to that may very well be: When the profit is taken out of the drug business.

TRIALS AND OTHER TRIBULATIONS

HOW HIGH WAS THE FENCE?

I first met Jim McNulty in 1947 when I attended the University of Arizona. We were both students and got to know one another over the four years, during which time we became friends. Jim's girlfriend was Jacqueline Boevers, who hailed from Wikieup, Arizona. Jacquie and I were both political science majors and attended a few classes together. She was very bright and an attractive young lady.

Jim, by his own admission a liberal Boston Irish-Catholic, was a friendly and gregarious man who loved people. He attended law school at the University of Arizona where he made many friends and became well known. He was involved in student body politics. After graduating, he was admitted to practice law in Arizona.

Jim joined the law firm of Gentry, McNulty and Kimble in Bisbee. His partners were Martin Gentry and Bill Kimble. He and Bill had known each other for years and were "best man" at each other's weddings. Building a distinguished career, Jim served in the Arizona Senate, on the Arizona Board of Regents, and in the United States House of Representatives.

He and I practiced law in Cochise County for many years, he in Bisbee and I in Douglas. There was a story around the Cochise County courthouse which became legend, about a trial in which Jim was counsel for the plaintiff.

It seems that his client (we'll call him John Smith) was a neighbor of Bill Brown and, over a period of time, a dispute arose as to the common dividing line between their two properties. One thing led to another, and they wound up in court opposing each other over their boundary line.

Jim was questioning his adversary Brown on the witness stand. A jury was present, and Jim's line of questioning was directed to the parties' dividing line.

"Mr. Brown, let's talk a little bit about that boundary between you and your neighbor. Do you know where that line is?"

"Yes, I do."

"Have you and Mr. Smith had a dispute over that line?"

"Yes, we have, Mr. McNulty. That's why we're here today in court."

"Now, Mr. Brown, please tell the jury where that line is."

Mr. Brown by his description drew a mental picture of the line for the jury. Jim's questioning went off on another vein, then he came back to the boundary line.

"Now, Mr. Brown, isn't it true that there is a fence on the line that separates you and Mr. Smith?"

"No, Mr. McNulty. There is no fence there."

Disappointed in the answer, Jim went on to another line of questioning and returned a little later to the question of the boundary.

"Now, Mr. Brown, let's talk a little more about that fence between you and Mr. Smith."

"Mr. McNulty, I told you there was no fence."

Exasperated, McNulty launched, "Well, Mr. Brown, if there had been a fence there, tell the jury how high that fence would have been."

The jury guffawed, but they went on to render a verdict in favor of Jim's client.

MY SHINGLE

It was 1953, not long after General Van Fleet had negotiated a cease-fire with the North Koreans at Panmunjom and returned to the United States by way of Alaska.

Little Flower (Daisy) and I had returned home with our infant daughter, Elizabeth, after a two-year tour of duty with the army, thirteen months of which was served at Fort Richardson, Alaska. Baby Liz was born on September 12, 1952, at Elmendorf Air Force Base Hospital next to Fort Rich.

I was released from active duty at Ft. Lewis, Washington, in August of 1953, and Daisy, Liz, and I returned to civilian life in Douglas, where I got a job with Southern Arizona Auto Company "selling" used cars. We rented a small one-bedroom home without air cooling of any kind. It was August and dreadfully hot and uncomfortable.

I couldn't *give* those darn cars away, much less sell them. I worked for three very frustrating weeks, during which time I didn't sell a single one. After lunch one day in the Gadsden Hotel, Dad, Shelley Richey, and I went into Dad's office, where I watched them play gin rummy. There was the usual banter that goes on in a card game, during which Shelley asked me what I was doing. He had been a practicing lawyer in Douglas for several years. A veteran himself of the Second World War, he had been a first lieutenant in the tank corps, as had I.

I told Shelley that I was having a hard time trying to sell automobiles and was living off my army separation pay. I had left the service with the rank of first lieutenant and received $3,000 on separation–no small amount in those days. Here I was–an officer and a gentleman–with a wife, infant child, and a job which I couldn't turn into money.

Shelley said casually, "Benny, why don't you go to law school?"

"How in the world am I going to do that?" I asked.

"Well, you're entitled to the GI bill, and the government will actually pay you while you're going to school."

That was news to me. Dad chimed in, "I think that's a great idea."

After thinking for a few moments, I called Daisy at home and said, "Pack our bags. We're going to law school in Tucson."

I heard something like, "Whoopee!" and she had our bags packed before I got home.

We came to Tucson. I qualified under the GI bill and started classes in September. That was the smartest thing I ever did. It changed my life more than any other thing that I can think of other than my marriage to Daisy.

I attended law school for three years. Every weekday found me at school from 8:00 to 5:00, whether I had class or not. I attacked it as a job. Nights, except Saturdays, were for study from 7:00 until 9:00–little time for play.

Our second daughter, Diane, came along on December 27, 1955. After three years of intense study, I graduated in May of 1956, took the two-day bar exam on July 13 and 14, passed, and was sworn in before the Arizona Supreme Court on October 13, 1956.

Daisy, Liz, Diane, and I returned to Douglas, where I hung out my shingle. It has now hung for over 50 years, and I feel it's time to take it down, pack it away, and pursue new ventures.

A TRAIN RIDE TO REMEMBER

In 1960, Southern Pacific filed an action before the Interstate Commerce Commission (ICC) seeking permission to abandon service of its two principal passenger trains through Douglas, the Argonaut and Golden State Limited. By this time, Southern Pacific's north line through Willcox was in operation. With diminishing returns from the shipment of passengers, cattle, and copper, the company's bottom line did not reflect well, which motivated the railroad's desire to withdraw service.

I was contacted by the Douglas Chamber of Commerce, of which I was an active member, and asked to represent the chamber in opposing Southern Pacific's proposed curtailment of service. The proceedings were held before the ICC in Douglas. I agreed to the job, but without any fee. The chamber was broke, unable to pay me.

I filed an application for a license to practice before the commission, which was granted. Proceedings before the ICC were different from the normal practice of law, and I was required to study in order to learn its strangely different rules.

The hearings were conducted in the Justice of the Peace courtroom in the old city hall building on Tenth Street. Southern Pacific was represented by Evans, Kitchell & Jenckes, a highly competent and prominent law firm in Phoenix which had long represented the railroad. Earl Carroll of that firm (now a retired United States district judge living in Phoenix) represented Southern Pacific. Witnesses were brought from El Paso and other places to present the railroad's case.

Denman K. McNear was superintendent of the El Paso and Rio Grande division of Southern Pacific. He came with his team to present the railroad's case. They arrived in the company's business car, a lavishly outfitted rail car in which they traveled in style. It boasted its own air conditioning and refrigeration systems, cooking facilities, bedroom, dining room, and lounge with bar. A cook/porter was assigned to the car to provide the amenities to which the high-powered executives were accustomed.

It took several months for the ICC to review all the evidence and make its decision. During that time, Johnny Reynolds, one of Southern Pacific's supervisors at Douglas, approached me about a fishing trip, traveling on the Mexican railway to Nacozari, Sonora, seventy miles south of Douglas. McNear had passed word to Johnny that he wanted to take our group fishing in Nacozari in SP's business car. The car was parked on a siding in Douglas where the railroad people had stayed during the course of the proceedings, which had lasted four days.

Johnny and I made arrangements to invite superior court judge Bill Kimble, Phelps Dodge vice president and general manager Walter Lawson, Earl Carroll, and my father (Ben Williams, Sr.) to go on the trip. All had varying interests in Nacozari. Dad was a good customer of Southern Pacific, shipping three carloads of copper concentrates a week from his mining company in Nacozari to the Douglas smelter.

McNear brought with him from El Paso two tax-and-right-of-way people, who were delightful companions.

On the arranged date, we boarded the plush rail car in Agua Prieta, where it had been switched to the Mexican train that traveled to Nacozari on Thursdays. Once we were aboard and comfortably seated, Sam Jenkins, the porter, took our drink orders. Sam was a skillful and experienced bartender. It turned out he was an equally good cook, for he prepared several meals that were absolutely delicious.

The train trip was interesting and the countryside fascinating. We first passed through Cabullona about ten miles south of Agua Prieta. This was a favorite picnic ground for Agua Prieta natives. Its enormous and plentiful cottonwoods with a clear running stream which meandered through fine river sand provided an ideal oasis in which to play in the Sonoran Desert.

The train stopped briefly at Cabullona to load and unload a few passengers. The next stop was Fronteras where passengers, sheep, goats, and chickens got on and off. Vendors meanwhile sold soft drinks, tamales, empanadas (popovers) and pan dulce (sweet bread) to train passengers.

If you are wondering to what Fronteras owes its founding, you might never guess that it was once an old and important Spanish presidio, established in 1692 to protect settlers from marauding Indians.

Our next stop was Esqueda, a cattle ranching, farming, and mining community which supported a cantina with a pool table. This is the pueblo where the 1956 movie *Wetback Hound* was filmed. It was an Oscar-winning "best short subject" film, featuring Marvin and Warner Glenn, lion-hunting guides and prominent cattle ranchers from Cochise County. In the film, their horses were tethered to the hitching post at the cantina's entrance.

Not long after leaving Esqueda, the train stopped at Turicachi, a small colony, really not much more than a wide spot in the road. Turicachi did have, however, a leveled area where every Sunday its young men played baseball.

On several hillsides overlooking the little community were rock breastworks which had been hurriedly thrown up by Mexican federal soldiers when Pancho Villa and his troops marched from Nacozari on their way to Agua Prieta in 1915. The *federales* used the rock structures for defense to hide behind when firing on Villa's troops in the valley below.

Nacozari train depot, dignitaries in front of Jesús Garcia monument. Depot was also used for showing moving pictures Author attended a Mexican movie in a smoke-filled room in this building in 1938. *Photo courtesy of Arizona Historical Society/Tucson. AHS# 58753*

Our last stop was Nacozari, where we were met at the station by an old friend of my father, Chic Nations. Chic got his nickname because he came from Oklahoma and was part Chickasaw Indian. His appearance was decidedly Indian. When Sam opened the door to let us out, he was greeted by Chic, who literally scared the daylights out of him. Sam had never been to Mexico. On the ride down to Nacozari, we had told him stories about wild Indians who were still running around the country. We told Sam we might encounter them anywhere. Later I learned that Sam shut the door to that business car and didn't set foot outside until greeted by his Southern Pacific companions back in the United States.

Dad, Lawson, author and Bill Kimble in front of Harvey Gobel's manager's residence

Harvey Gobel, Phelps Dodge's manager at Nacozari, met us at the train station and directed the removal of our bags to the Phelps Dodge staff house. It was well appointed and

Dad and Harvey Gobel in the garden of the manager's residence

Dad, Walter Lawson, Johnny Reynolds,
author, taken at Nacozari Lake

served by two well-trained maids who doubled as cooks. Bottom line, we were not wanting in any respect. Our stay was memorable.

The following day, most of us went up to the little lake above Nacozari, which the local people called "El Guacal."

Another evening of fun and frivolity followed with lots to eat and drink and good times. During the night, there came a terrible rain storm between Agua Prieta and Nacozari. It washed out two railway bridges, so the train on which we were to return couldn't make it. Arrangements were made for us to go to Agua Prieta on what was called the *auto-via,* a self-propelled rail car which took us to the washed-out bridge. Here we were met by a Jeep-like vehicle with flanged steel wheels which fit on the rails and rode on rubber tires. You

James Douglas memorial fountain in the plaza at Nacozari

might think this would be a comfortable ride, but it wasn't. We used this method to cross the creek bed where the bridges had washed out. On the other side of each washout we were met by a small railroad maintenance car which had a motor and hand pump, either of which could be used to propel the vehicle. You have probably seen such handcars in old movies and cartoons. This was a really rough ride.

Sam had to stay in Nacozari in the business car for ten days until the bridges were rebuilt so the train could come out. He was the happiest man in the world to get out of Mexico, away from all those "hostiles."

Now, if you want a ride on the SP, you'll have to catch it in Willcox, because they just flat dropped Douglas.

A MATTER OF PERSPECTIVE

Dale Fenter was my law partner in Douglas in the early 1960s. Our law office was in the professional building across the street from the post office on Tenth Street.

Dale was a great law partner, with good common sense, a firm grasp of the law, and a keen sense of humor.

I recall a trial involving damages allegedly caused by an earthen dam which spread flood waters from its natural watercourse during heavy rains. It had been built in the eastern foothills of the Chiricahua Mountains near Portal, Arizona.

The legal question was whether or not the structure had diverted water out of its natural course, casting it onto a neighboring landowner's property and causing damage to land and buildings.

The trial was held in Bisbee before Judge Anthony T. Deddens. Tony had come back to Cochise County from Maricopa County, where he had practiced for several years and served as president of the Arizona State Bar. He was a judge who made quick decisions, not always right, and upon whose shoulders the black robe of justice weighed heavily.

Phil Toci represented the defendant, and Dale represented the plaintiff. The trial lasted for two days, with a number of witnesses for both parties.

Toward the end of the second day, both plaintiff and defendant rested their cases. At that time, Dale requested that the judge fly with him to view the watercourse that had been the subject of the dispute. (Dale had recently learned to fly and had logged approximately 100 hours as a pilot.)

"Mr. Fenter, I am not aware of any legal precedent for such a viewing. I must see some law on the matter. Please prepare a memorandum and have it ready for me tomorrow morning at 9 o'clock. At that time I will rule on the propriety of the court flying with you to look over the premises."

After the judge declared the evening recess and retired to his chambers, Phil Toci turned to Dale. "You know that damned blind, old judge wouldn't recognize a watercourse if you were to rub his nose in it! Good luck with your memorandum. I'll see you in the morning."

That evening, working like a beaver, Dale did his research, found a couple of cases which established a precedent, and prepared a memorandum and argument sustaining his position that the court could view the premises. Dale felt that the memorandum was not completely convincing to establish his point of view, but it was the best he could do.

Remembering what Phil Toci had said about the judge, Dale decided to prepare another memorandum. In this second memorandum, he said, "Notwithstanding that after Your Honor left the courtroom, Mr. Toci stated, 'You know that damned blind, old judge wouldn't recognize a watercourse if you were to rub his nose in it,' plaintiff feels that a view from the air will quickly reveal plaintiff's right to recovery."

When court convened the following morning, the judge stated, "Gentlemen, I will now hear your final arguments, but before you begin, I want to see Mr. Fenter's legal memorandum in support of the question of whether or not the court should view the premises from the air."

Dale approached the bench and placed before the judge the real memorandum dealing with the law. He placed a copy of the phony memorandum on Toci's counsel table.

Dale sat down, waiting for the judge to read his memorandum and issue a ruling. At the same time, Phil Toci read the second memorandum that Dale had placed on his table, turned seven shades of crimson red and began carefully watching the judge, who continued to read the true memorandum.

Toci turned to Dale and whispered, "You dirty so-and-so. I would never have said such a thing if I had known you were going to put it in a legal memorandum."

Dale merely smiled.

Upon completing his review of the memorandum, the judge stated, "Mr. Fenter, your memorandum is well done, but I see no compelling reason for me to get in that airplane with you and view the premises. Your request is denied."

By this time, Toci figured out he had been tricked.

Both parties proceeded with their final arguments, and a judgment was rendered in favor of the defendant, denying any damage caused by plaintiff's dam.

Even though he won the case, Toci was so mad at Dale that he didn't speak to him for months.

A LITTLE WHITE LIE

"Mayor, what can we do? The cows are getting through the fence and onto the golf course greens and tearing them up."

Challenged by this question, I recalled how hard the club members and city workforce had labored to get the golf course and greens into the fine condition that they were when Bill DaVee, my city manager, and Benny LaForge, my director of public works, posed the question to me.

The city owned and partially supported the nine-hole golf course located on Leslie Canyon Road north of Douglas and adjacent to the Cochise County Fairgrounds.

The Douglas Golf and Social Club, which operated the golf club for a number of years as a private enterprise, while at the same time maintaining a municipal golfing facility, had obtained a commitment from the city for $80,000 with which to purchase valves, water lines, connections and timers in order to provide more grass and create a better golf course.

Many club members had volunteered their time and talents to dig the ditches, lay the waterlines and make all required connections. It made a big project for the members, who for the most part could work only after normal work hours and on weekends. Some members worked a number of days, taking off the time required from their own work.

An architect was hired to prepare drawings and specifications for the new water system, and it was placed in operation. It was amazing how the grass flourished on the old hardpan dirt fairways.

Kenny Sugarman, a greenskeeper with proven abilities, had been hired away from Sun Sites and given the assignment of improving the course to make it a more topflight facility. He even moved a mobile home onto the facility and lived on the premises.

After the challenging question from Bill and Benny, we discussed the problem. They told me that our course, although fenced from the neighboring ranchers, was being invaded by cows belonging to one of them in particular whose cattle really liked the fresh, green grass our course and greens provided.

The rancher had been asked a number of times to fence his place so his cows couldn't destroy our greens. Each time the cattle walked on the spongy greens, they left deep hoof prints, which of course made putting impossible.

Bill and Benny were at wits' end and wanted to know if the city should bring a lawsuit against the rancher to keep his cattle off the course.

"You write and send a registered letter to that guy," I said, "advising him that on a particular date, approximately two weeks from the date of the letter, the club is going to spray the greens with an extremely toxic insecticide which in the past has proven fatal to livestock."

Of course, there was no intention of putting such a formula on the lush green grass, but the thought might induce the rancher to fix his fence.

After a week passed, I asked Bill what was going on, and he told me the rancher had worked like a beaver fixing his fence, and no cattle had trespassed onto the golf course.

There was no further trouble with cattle trespassing, and the course improved until it was in prime condition and enjoyed by golfers from Douglas, Agua Prieta, and surrounding areas.

FLYING HIGH

What a Circus
"What if They Shoot?"
The Nail Polish Case

FLYING HIGH

During the 1970s, while practicing law in Douglas, I got involved in recovering airplanes that had been stolen in the United States and ended up in Mexico. I became quite adept at the process, eventually recovering twenty-one airplanes.

In 1974, I conducted a seminar in El Paso for fifty people who wanted to learn how to retrieve stolen airplanes. The seminar was so successful that I was invited to go to Washington, D.C., to brief our State Department. At that time, our government was negotiating a new treaty with Mexico relating to stolen aircraft, motor vehicles, and marine craft. Senator Barry Goldwater recommended that I serve on the United States section of the committee, which was chaired by Senator Charles Percy of Illinois. Ultimately the committee's conclusions were adopted by both governments, and form the current treaty in existence between Mexico and the United States.

Here are the stories of three of those airplanes that I recovered.

WHAT A CIRCUS!

In the 1970s, Ringling Brothers circus came to town and set up behind the YMCA building west of the railroad tracks in Douglas. This had been their usual spot for thirty years. There was much hoopla, including a parade down G Avenue, the main street of Douglas, with elephants, lions, and tigers in cages on wagons. Much fanfare. Posters everywhere. Newspaper coverage. Radio announcements every fifteen minutes. You couldn't miss the fact that the circus was in town.

My daughters, Liz and Diane, were ecstatic, so on the appointed day, we went to the circus grounds, bought our tickets, and sat down on the wooden benches set up under the big top to watch the show.

Shortly after we were seated, Eddie Price, a friend, sought me out, tapped me on the shoulder and excitedly told me, "Doc Still is under arrest and his airplane has been impounded. You've got to come get him out!"

"Where is he?"

"He's in Agua Prieta in the Mexican customs office."

Doc Still had been a good friend of mine for many years. Shelley Richey, Dr. Montgomery, Ed Huxtable, and I had visited at his home in Littlefield, Texas, where he hosted a cocktail party–in a dry county by the way–and took us on a marvelous bobwhite and pheasant hunt. All of us flew to Littlefield in a Bonanza piloted by Ed Huxtable, who also liked to hunt. Ed had been a navy pilot in the

191

Second World War and was shot down twice in the Battle of Midway. During the battle, Ed ditched two planes in the drink—a real navy flying hero, as well as a great pilot.

After the circus performance ended, I took the kids home, then drove to Agua Prieta. Sure enough, there was Doc Still in custody. "They arrested me right in my boat while I was fishing with Shelley. They took me off at pistol point."

"Who took you off the lake?"

"Mexican customs. They were armed with pistols and brought their boat right up to mine and pointed their pistols at me like I was public enemy number one. They made me get in their boat. Shelley said, 'Don't worry, Jack, I'll take care of your boat. Call Benny. If anybody can help, he can.' They took me off the lake up to the airstrip and flew me back up here to Agua Prieta under arrest."

It was evening by then, and getting cold. Doc was in short pants. The Mexicans wouldn't let him change to warmer clothes, and it looked like he was going to spend the night in a Mexican jail.

In those days, I represented the Mexican consul at Douglas, and I was able to enlist his aid in the release of Doc overnight, with the promise that we would return the following morning.

I asked Doc, "Why were you arrested?"

"I didn't have papers for my plane."

Flying a plane into Mexico without checking with Mexican customs is a serious breach of Mexican law, and Doc's beautiful Bonanza airplane had been confiscated and flown to Agua Prieta by Mexican customs, where it was in the municipal hangar under seizure and being guarded by two soldiers armed with rifles.

I contacted Consul Jimenez again and asked him if there was anything he could do to help recover the plane. He agreed to help.

The next morning, Doc Still appeared at the office of Mexican customs at the designated time. He was assessed a fine of $100, nominal under the circumstances, and his plane was released.

Later, I asked the consul what the fee was. "A case of Chivas Regal."

Who got the Chivas Regal, I'll never know and really don't care, but it sure greased the skids for the release of the plane and Doc Still.

Getting my friend and his plane out of the hands of the *federales* was as almost as much fun as going to the circus.

"WHAT IF THEY SHOOT?"

"What's your problem?" I asked.

It was one evening after work in 1970. I was at the local "attitude adjustment" facility located in the Gadsden Hotel in Douglas. While I was enjoying a cool one with friends, two men approached me.

"Are you Ben Williams, the lawyer?"

"In the flesh," I answered.

"We work for AVEMCO Aircraft Insurance Group of Bethesda, Maryland, and we need to recover a plane that's being held by authorities in Mexico. We've been told that if anybody around these parts can help us get that plane back, it's you. Is that true?"

"Well, I don't know. I want to learn more of the details. Come to my office here in the hotel at nine tomorrow morning."

"Okay, we'll see you tomorrow."

Sure enough, Tom Carpenter and Bill Swift appeared the next morning at nine. They announced to my assistant, Edna Inglehart, who they were and that they had an appointment to see me. Edna buzzed me on the intercom. I went to the outer office, greeted Tom and Bill, and showed them into my inner sanctum. My office was just off the north lobby entrance, small but well decorated. The chairs were leather. "Marble" was the brand, very expensive, with a walnut finish. Two walls lined with walnut shelves contained impressive leather-bound law books, old and well-worn through much use. One wall was comprised of a large window covered by draw drapes, which when opened looked into the lobby of the hotel.

My soon-to-be clients sat down in the chairs across from my desk. Tom was a big guy with sandy hair, well dressed in a grey suit, and articulate. He had a New England accent but had, I learned, gone to Princeton. Bill was short and stocky, and he spoke with a Texas accent. He had attended Texas A&M. Tom was the spokesman. He told me they were both from the main AVEMCO office in Bethesda. They had made four trips to Douglas and Agua Prieta and had paid $1,000 to a Mexican who told them he could get the plane released for them. Eighteen months of unproductive frustration showed in their faces.

Tom began by telling me of the theft of a Cessna Model 337 Skymaster airplane, which their company had insured. It was stolen from an airport in Dallas and flown to Mexico illegally, where it had been used to fly drugs and contraband until seized by Mexican customs and impounded in Agua Prieta. The Skymaster is a twin-fuselage aircraft with a large cargo compartment. The plane is powered by two engines. It has been better described as a twin-engine "centerline thrust" aircraft–an unusual design for private aircraft with one engine pushing and one engine pulling. They told me the Skymaster had been in commercial production since late 1963. Tom related that someone had walked up to the 337, which was parked among a number of other planes, released the tie-downs, opened the cabin door, got in, started the engines, and flew off while nobody was watching.

I asked how it was that the plane had been so easily stolen and was told that in those days, Cessna used keys that could fit any number of aircraft. Somebody with a ring of Cessna keys could go down the flight line and open almost any Cessna.

AVEMCO had paid off the owner and wanted to recover the plane to minimize its losses. The plane reportedly crossed illegally into Mexico and was flown a number of times before Mexican authorities seized it. It had an "N" number (N501T), which signified American registration. Someone had reported the "N" number to AOPA (Aircraft Owners and Pilots Association), an American organization that maintains a list of stolen aircraft by registration numbers.

Tom and Bill told me of their many unfruitful efforts to recover the plane, talking to people in Mexico, paying money, going to the Mexican customs office, even to the United States consulate in Hermosillo. I advised them that they were Americans without business visas and, as such, had no legal identity in Mexico. They could not make official inquiries or appearances before Mexican tribunals. They were nonentities, and Mexican officials treated them as such.

After talking as we did, they said, "Will you help us get the plane?"

"Sure."

"What will it take?"

"Give me a retainer of $2,500 and I'll see what I can do. I have a friend who is a Mexican lawyer on the other side of the border. He might be able to help."

Tom gave me a check for $2,500, after which I went to Agua Prieta to talk to Licenciado Carlos Gonzales. His office was very neat and professional looking, even though it needed a new paint job and new furniture. His typewriter was an old manual Underwood exposed-key upright, not state-of-the-art even in those days. "Adequate" describes the office.

I had known Carlos for several years, and we had worked on a couple of cases together. He was effective and competent in my book, and I trusted him. He had the familiar moustache worn by most Hispanic men. Carlos had been educated at the University of Sonora Law School in Hermosillo. He dressed in a suit and tie and looked like a lawyer. We spoke in Spanish. Although he understood English, he was more comfortable speaking in his native tongue.

Carlos said, "I'll look into the matter and call you."

"Fine. Let me know what it will take to get the plane, if we can get it at all."

"Okay."

"May I pay you something now?"

"No, let me look into it first."

A couple of days later he called and said, "Bring me $5,000 in $50 bills and I'll get the plane released for you."

I returned to my office in the Gadsden, called Tom Carpenter in Bethesda, and told him I needed $5,000. He wired the money that afternoon, after which I went to the Bank of Douglas, where I got $50 bills. Later in the afternoon, I put the bills in the casing of a spare tire in the trunk of my car and drove to my friend's office in Agua Prieta, where I gave him the cash.

The aircraft was hangared in the Agua Prieta Municipal Airport, which was nothing more than a big building open at one end, with a gas pump and a dirt runway alongside. I personally went to the hangar to see what the plane looked like and found that there were two Mexican soldiers armed with automatic rifles guarding it. I didn't go beyond the door of the hangar because I didn't want the soldiers to know I was interested in the Skymaster. There were three or four other planes in the hangar so they didn't know which plane I was interested in. One quick look, and I left.

When I took the money to Carlos, he told me to have a pilot at the airport the following morning at first light. The pilot was to taxi the aircraft out of the hangar and take off.

Later that day, I hired a pilot and instructed him to be at the airport at dawn to fly the Skymaster from Agua Prieta to Bisbee-Douglas International Airport. Bill Curtis was an experienced pilot living in Douglas. He had been flying charter for more than twenty years around southern Arizona and northern Mexico. Bill had flown me a couple of times to Dad's tungsten mine on the Yaqui River 200 miles south of Douglas in a very remote mountainous area in Sonora. Also, Bill had flown me and many other American fishermen to Novillo Lake east of Hermosillo. He was experienced and knowledgeable about border flying. He also understood Spanish. I told Bill about the soldiers but said they wouldn't be looking when he cranked up the engines and taxied out of the hangar onto the airstrip.

"How do you know? What if they shoot?" he asked.

"Don't worry, they won't see you."

"That's easy for you to say."

"Well, some things just have to be accepted on blind faith," I retorted. "You want the job? I bet they won't shoot. Want to take the gamble? The pay is good. It's a piece of cake," I said. "$350 for a morning's work." That amount was a handsome sum in 1970.

"If they shoot me, promise me you won't let them bury my body in old Mexico."

"I promise."

The plane had to be flown to Bisbee-Douglas International, nine miles north of Douglas, because that was the official port of entry where U.S. Customs and

Immigration made inspections of aircraft coming into the United States.

I notified customs that the plane had probably been carrying arms and marijuana and was coming over to BDI. They told me, "When the plane is airborne, call us at the Douglas Port of Entry and we'll dispatch an agent to BDI. Instruct the pilot and all passengers aboard that they are not to set foot on the ground after the plane lands until our agent comes to inspect the aircraft."

I did as instructed, then went to the airport to await arrival of the plane. It landed without incident. The U.S. authorities inspected it and then released it to my custody. I returned to my office and called AVEMCO to advise them of the release and tell them that it was now "their baby."

Bill Curtis came to my office that afternoon to collect his pay.

"How did it go?" I asked.

"Well, I had a friend drop me at the airport. It was still dark, just beginning to show light. The plane was in the back of the hangar. There were two Mexican solders with rifles slung over their shoulders. They were talking and one was smoking a cigarette. They looked at me but said nothing. I walked to the plane as if I owned it, glancing out of the corner of my eye to see if they were taking their rifles off their shoulders to challenge me. I proceeded to unlock the plane's cabin door with the key you had given me. (Tom had left me the keys for the plane.)

"The guards acted as if I was not there. I had my heart in my throat as I inserted the key in the ignition, expecting at any instant to hear a shot and see a bullet hole in the windshield. Nothing happened. I started first one engine and then the other. They both caught on the first crank. I taxied toward the hangar door past the guards, wondering when they were going to fire at me. Again, nothing happened, so I taxied out of the hangar and onto the strip for takeoff. No shots or bullets. I gunned the engines and took off for BDI. Once airborne, I turned the radio on. It worked, so I radioed, 'BDI, this is November 501 Tango airborne from Mexico, bound for BDI. Request permission to land. ETA 0630 hours.'

"'Roger, November 501 Tango. Use runway 21. When you have parked your aircraft, do not deplane until U.S. Customs arrives to clear you.'

"'Roger, BDI. This is November 501 Tango out.'"

Later, in a phone conversation with Tom at AVEMCO, he asked about the guards who were watching the plane.

"They were looking the other way when my pilot took off," I replied.

Elated, he asked if I would be interested in recovering other planes. AVEMCO had a list of stolen aircraft believed to have been flown to Mexico.

I told them I was very interested, and with that commenced a lucrative practice in airplane recovery.

I have often wondered who shared in the division of the $5,000. But as the saying goes: "Don't ask, don't tell."

THE NAIL POLISH CASE

In June of 1974, I received a phone call from Tom Carpenter of AVEMCO asking if I would help recover a Cessna 172 which had been stolen from its owner in Kansas Settlement south of Willcox, Arizona.

The owner, Cecil Miller, grew maize, cotton, and corn. He had a 640-acre farm and was a successful farmer. He had built a hangar next to his farmhouse for his plane. The hangar was completely open at one end so that anybody who wanted to could walk right in.

"Walk right in" is exactly what somebody did in April of 1974, unlocking the plane with a key. In those days a ring of assorted Cessna keys could open any number of their planes. The thief had obviously watched the hangar to determine when it was unattended. He entered, started the engine, and flew off to Mexico.

AVEMCO had taken a bill of sale from Cecil Miller after paying him for his loss.

The aircraft's registration number was November 6101 Quebec (N6101Q). Somebody had seen it parked in a military impoundment lot at Rocky Point (Puerto Peñasco), Mexico, and reported its location to AOPA (Aircraft Owners and Pilots Association) in Frederick, Maryland, where AOPA kept a registry of stolen aircraft.

Although in recent years Rocky Point has become a popular, high-class tourist resort, with plenty of fine hotels, restaurants, and tourist facilities, in 1974 it was a sleepy Mexican fishing village.

The plane was under Mexican government seizure and would not be released without official authorization from the Mexican attorney general in Mexico City.

At the impoundment site, two Mexican sailors armed with automatic rifles guarded the plane. The enclosure was built of railroad ties and barbed wire–sufficiently large so that no one could get close to the aircraft, which was parked in the center of the lot under some tamarisk trees. The compound was located just north of town.

"Ben, you were able to recover that plane for us in Agua Prieta. Do you think you can get this one also? We've already paid the owner for his loss, and the plane's now ours."

"Tom, I'd sure like to take a shot at it. Send me documents showing AVEMCO's ownership and an executed power of attorney designating me as your agent, and I'll go to work. I'll also need a retainer of $2,500 to start the ball rolling."

"Jump on it, Ben. Please keep me informed of your progress."

I set about my duties, first obtaining from the FAA an official certified document proving ownership. It showed that Cecil Miller of Cochise County, Arizona, owned the plane. I presented this, along with a certified copy of the bill of sale from Miller to AVEMCO, to a competent English-Spanish interpreter, who interpreted the two documents and certified the correctness of their translation. I notarized the documents and sent them to the Cochise County clerk's office at Bisbee for authentication of the fact that I was a duly licensed and qualified notary public. This bore the official seal of the clerk of the court.

I then obtained from the Cochise County sheriff's office a certified copy of the report of theft, which I had translated and certified. This became part of the package I presented to the United States Embassy in Mexico City for its review. It was also given to the Mexican attorney general along with an official request for an order directed to all Mexican authorities, state and federal, ordering the release of the aircraft to me upon due proof of my identity.

At the local stationery store, I bought some gold seals and red ribbon, along with a device with which to permanently attach the ribbons and seals to my packet of documents to make it look very official. This added nothing to the legal status of the documents, but it seemed to impress the Mexican authorities when they reviewed them.

Preparing and assembling the package took a great deal of time. In the meantime, Tom Carpenter was calling me every two weeks from Bethesda asking for written updates. His constant calling finally became such a pain in the neck that I finally told him, "Look, I'll contact you when I have something to report. In the meantime, please don't waste your time and mine by asking for meaningless reports."

After a wait of eight months, I received a package from the Mexican attorney general's office containing a written order directing that the aircraft be released to me. Prior to receiving the official order of release, I made an exploratory trip to Puerto Peñasco to look at the plane to see what was needed in order to fly it back to the United States. I made this trip in November of 1976 and took with me a good friend, husband of my legal secretary, Natalia Vasquez. Mike Vasquez and I went to Peñasco in my Jeep Wagoneer. On arriving in Rocky Point, we went to the office of Capitán Xavier Ortiz of the Mexican Navy, who was military commander of the port. Custody of the seized plane fell under his jurisdiction.

Prior to going to his office, however, I drove with Mike right up to the fenced compound for a good look at the plane. Mike was scared and hollered, "For God's sake, Ben, don't get too close. One of those SOBs might shoot us."

"Mike, I don't think they'll shoot unless we try to go through the fence. After we get a peek at the plane, we'll hightail it out of here."

After viewing the plane, I went to Captain Ortiz's office, which was the usual old, smelly Mexican government office. It hadn't been painted in a number of years and contained some oak furniture that looked like it had gone through the Mexican Revolution of 1910. Captain Ortiz received me graciously. I identified myself and told him that I was interested in the recovery of the airplane for its owner.

He seemed to hesitate, and then told me in Spanish (giving no indication that he understood English) that the plane had been sitting in the enclosure for a number of months. By his hesitation, I thought he was after a *mordida* (bribe). I suggested to him that if money would help expedite the plane's release, arrangements could be made.

"Licenciado Williams, you may not realize it, but you have attempted to bribe a Mexican federal officer. I am going to overlook it this time, but I want you to know it is a very serious crime in Mexico to bribe a government official. You could be prosecuted."

I almost fell dead from surprise, never before having encountered a Mexican officer so honest, enthusiastic, and dedicated in his enforcement of the law.

I asked Captain Ortiz how it was that the Mexicans got custody of the plane, and he told me a fascinating story.

"Mexican customs was alerted to the fact that this plane was involved in smuggling marijuana into the United States and returning to Mexico with illegal guns and electronics."

The Mexicans in another airplane had laid chase to the Cessna when it was spotted. At the time, it was loaded with marijuana. On approaching Rocky Point with the Mexican officials in pursuit, bales of marijuana were thrown out of the plane, several dropping in the yards of poor Mexican peons, who realized they were suddenly rich. The fleeing Americans crash-landed the Cessna in the desert east of Rocky Point and fled on foot into the Sonoran Desert.

"Did the authorities pursue these two guys?" I asked.

"No. We knew there was no place for them to go in the desert. Sure enough, after a day and a half out there without anything to eat or drink, they came dragging into town. They were desperate, begging for water and food, and were so glad to see somebody that they didn't care if they went to jail or not. They were convicted of violations of Mexican law and are currently in the penitentiary at Hermosillo.

"Would you like to see the plane, Mr. Williams?"

"Yes, sir."

Upon entering the compound and seeing the plane, I noticed that the registration numbers were different. Instead of November 6101 (N6101Q) Quebec, it was November 5101 Oboe (N5101O).

"Captain Ortiz, this is not our plane," I sadly proclaimed.

I was heartbroken to think about all the valuable time and hard work that had been wasted.

"Come up close and I'll show you the serial number inside the door."

He unlocked the cabin door and we looked inside. There stamped into the metal frame was a serial number, N6101Q, clear as day.

Captain Ortiz then said, "Licenciado, look closely at these painted-on numbers."

Someone had repainted the 6 to look like a 5 and the Q to look like an O–apparently done with fingernail polish, and in a hurry.

After I examined the plane, I told Ortiz I would return with an order from the Mexican attorney general directing the plane's release. We returned to our motel, where Mike and I got our things and then drove back to Douglas.

About this time, I met an American who lived in Tijuana, Baja California, by the name of Jack Devine. His business was recovering stolen automobiles and airplanes from Mexico. Jack was a soldier-of-fortune type who was possessed of a most pleasing personality. He was completely conversant in both Spanish and English. Married to a Mexican woman, the two of them had lived in Tijuana for several years. He and I teamed up, with the understanding that I would do the paperwork and he would do whatever was physically necessary to get the plane back to the United States.

Jack employed two young men named Virgil and Frank Kelly, who lived just outside San Diego. Both were excellent aviation mechanics and pilots, and fearless. They could fly a broomstick if you put a motor, a tail, and a wing on the darned thing.

Jack flew to Rocky Point along with the Kelly brothers in Jack's plane to look over the craft, with the idea of getting it in flying condition for the flight out of Mexico.

Jack told me that when I went down with the order of release, I should bring a 55-gallon drum of aviation gas, along with a magneto and a new propeller. The old propeller had been broken when the plane crash-landed in the desert.

Four months after my reconnaissance trip to Peñasco, I received an official letter from the United States consulate at Hermosillo enclosing an order of the Mexican attorney general directing the release of the plane to me. The United States embassy in Mexico City had forwarded the document to the consulate in Hermosillo to give to me.

Armed with the official release, I again contacted Mike, rounded up the aviation gas, magneto, and propeller and loaded them in my Jeep, and we were off to

Rocky Point. I called Jack, who contacted the Kelly brothers, and we all met in Rocky Point.

The Kellys looked the plane over and said that there would be no problem to get it to fly. They had some WD40 with them and took the head off the engine, squirted WD40 into the cylinders, attached the propeller, filled the plane with gas, and cranked the propeller. The engine sputtered once

Author and plane after order of release was issued by attorney general of Mexico

before it caught, then began running like a new sewing machine.

Mike Vasquez in front of author's jeep at Rocky Point

Mike and I headed back home to Douglas. The Kellys flew the plane out the next day from Rocky Point, heading for a small airfield just outside San Diego.

The next morning, I received a telephone call from Jack telling me that Mexican customs had forced our plane down at

Mexicali, where it was again under seizure. They claimed there were marijuana seeds in the plane. I knew this to be a scam and an excuse to pry a big mordida out of us.

"Jack, you tell those SOBs that if there are any marijuana seeds in the plane, they put them there, because the plane was inspected thoroughly by Mexican authorities at Rocky Point and released. It was in flight from Rocky Point to San Diego when it was forced down by those SOBs at Mexicali. Let me know if there are any more problems, and I'll contact the U.S. Consulate to intervene with the Mexican attorney general."

Jack did as I suggested; the plane was released and flew on to San Diego. Once the plane entered the United States, I contacted Tom Carpenter at AVEMCO and told him we had the plane in San Diego. It had been a long and complicated exercise, but we were able to get it back, and AVEMCO minimized its loss when it sold the plane.

Such is the story of the Nail Polish Case.

Jack Devine and author on another airplane recovery

OFFICIALLY YOURS

LOVE LETTERS

In 1953, while serving with the 518th Military Police Company on temporary duty from my regular duties as a tank platoon leader, I was designated post officer of the day.

I was a first lieutenant stationed at Fort Richardson, Alaska, and after normal duty hours, I had retired to my on-post quarters where I lived with my wife, Daisy, and daughter, Elizabeth.

No sooner had we finished dinner than I got a telephone call from Sergeant Gibbens, the desk sergeant at the provost marshal's office. He told me there was a problem that he felt I should handle. I was lounging in my quarters and really not eager to get out on the cold Alaskan night to go to the office where the good sergeant was "holding the fort." I told Gibbens to go ahead and handle the matter himself.

"Lieutenant, I feel this is going to require your help. It is beyond my capability."

"All right, Sergeant. I'll be down shortly."

When I arrived at the provost marshal's office, Sergeant Gibbens introduced me to Sally Swanson, a young woman eighteen years of age, who was distraught and crying beyond control. Tears were flowing down her face and she could barely catch her breath. She was unable to tell me what had happened. I was fearful that she had sustained a serious physical injury of some sort, when Sergeant Gibbens said, "Lieutenant, Miss Swanson here came all the way up here from Alabama to get married to Private Casey, who is assigned to the 95th Light Tank Company. Lieutenant, didn't you come from the 95th?"

"Indeed I did, Sergeant, although I didn't know Private Casey."

"Well, it seems that a Corporal Ross has been writing Casey's letters because Casey can't read or write. There've been a number of letters back and forth, and in his last letter, Ross told Miss Swanson that Casey wanted to marry her, that he was deeply in love with her and had set a wedding date for the fifteenth of April at the post chapel. Chaplain O'Leary, according to Miss Swanson, is to tie the knot, and all details for the wedding ceremony and honeymoon have been arranged by Casey.

Author in Alaska when serving as officer of the day

Author and Captain John Kwock, both provost marshal's office, Fort Richardson, Alaska

"When Miss Swanson arrived on Northwest Airlines, she took a cab out here to Fort Rich and telephoned Casey at the 95th. Casey said he didn't know what she was talking about and refused to come in and see her. He said someone had made a big mistake. He confessed that Corporal Ross had been writing his letters for him and said he didn't know what was in the letters because he couldn't read or write. Corporal Ross had been reading Miss Swanson's letters to Casey when they arrived.

"Miss Swanson broke down and didn't know what to do. Someone referred her here to the duty desk. So now, Lieutenant, what do we do?"

"Well, we've got a real mess here, Sergeant."

I spoke to Miss Swanson and told her that the best thing the army could do was call the Red Cross and have them make arrangements for her return to Alabama. I told Gibbens to get the local representative of the Red Cross and make contact so they could take over and get Miss Swanson back to her home.

The next morning, I summoned Private Casey to my office early in the morning and told him he'd better not get involved in another mess like that or he was sure to be court-martialed. I didn't know what grounds we could court-martial him on, but I thought that the mere threat would be adequate. Further, I admonished him that he was not to get involved in writing any more love letters until he learned to read and write. Further, that there was a class on post to teach GIs how to read and write, and he'd better darn well sign up for it.

Well, so much for twenty-four hours of "routine duty" as officer of the day. The moral of the story: Be careful what you write or what you let somebody else write for you, as it can come back to bite you on the behind.

THE COMPANY PORTRAIT
(THE QUIET PHOTOGRAPH)

How good is your hearing? Mine is nothing to brag about.

My hearing loss first became noticeable when I was a University of Arizona ROTC cadet attending summer training at Camp Hood, Texas. After firing practice on the rifle and tank cannon ranges, my ears rang like bells–so loud I could barely hear. With the passage of time, most of the ringing stopped, but my hearing has progressively worsened.

In 1970, after having practiced law in Douglas since 1956, I was elected to the board of directors of Arizona Public Service Company (APS), a large public utility which supplied electricity and natural gas to most of Arizona. One of the first things I was told to do as a new director was have my portrait made to hang in the board meeting room in the APS building. Markow Studios of Phoenix made the portrait. It was approximately two feet by three feet and done in color.

Not knowing any better, I appeared at the time designated for my sitting wearing a powder blue suit with light blue tie and sideburns almost down to my neck. Just thirty-nine years of age, I was the youngest member of the board.

The portrait was made, and it was hung in the board meeting room along with pictures of the other sixteen directors. I must say it was a vivid contrast compared to those of the distinguished persons wearing dark suits and red ties for the most part. I later learned that for public photographs or portraits, one should wear dark

215

clothes and preferably a red or blue tie. If you notice on television, most distinguished male personages appear in like dress.

For several years, I sat in the board room looking at my not-so-handsome portrait. It really clashed with the other highly proper-looking portraits. Finally, I could stand it no longer and asked if I could have another portrait made to replace my original picture. I was told, "Of course."

By that time, the company had its own photo studio in the company building at 411 North Central in Phoenix. An appointment was made for me. I appeared at 9:00 o'clock on a Thursday morning, this time attired in a dark blue suit, white shirt, red tie, and without long sideburns.

Upon my arrival, I was greeted with, "Mr. Williams, it will take us just a few minutes to prepare the studio for your sitting. Please sit down in the waiting room, make yourself comfortable, and enjoy a magazine while we arrange the furniture and lighting."

I thanked them, sat down, and proceeded to read a magazine. I read for fifteen minutes. Nobody came to announce they were ready for my sitting. I thought, "Well, they're just taking a long time to arrange the studio, so I'll wait a little longer."

Another ten minutes passed and no one had come out to inform me that they were ready. I became impatient and headed back into the studio. As I walked in, I was met by the photographer. "Mr. Williams, are you still here?"

"Certainly I'm still here. Where have you been?"

He asked in surprise, "Mr. Williams, where did *you* go when the fire alarm sounded?"

I was dumbfounded. I didn't hear the alarm causing everyone to leave the building.

My portrait was duly made, and I was pleased with the result. It hung in the board room until my retirement in 2000 after a total of thirty years of service.

TOUR OF DUTY

I was taken out of reserve and placed on active duty on June 17, 1980. At the same time, I was assigned to a new boss, Ben Williams, Jr. He and I went through some fascinating campaigns and saw some heavy action at times. We were to serve together for four hitches. I am retired now and enjoying the life of Reilly, but I feel I must tell you my story.

At first, my new CO appeared to be a little hesitant–there was a slight tremor in his hand. However, as time went on he gained confidence in my ability to command along with him, and we became good comrades. His tremor went away. At first, under our joint command, the troops were a little apprehensive as to how well we would perform. Our command numbered 13,000 and later, before our retirement, this increased to 15,000, almost the size of a division. By now, you may have guessed that our command was comprised of the city of Douglas, with six elected aldermen to assist. We were located in southeast Arizona, right on the U.S.-Mexico border.

In 1982, my CO pressed me into additional service when he chaired the elected Freeholders who drafted the new charter for the city. Being chairman was tough duty, because it entailed many hours of planning and most of it was night fighting, sometimes with little quarter given. However, after eight weeks of intense duty, a compromise was reached and the fourteen Freeholders signed the new charter with only one abstaining.

After our first skirmishes, Ben and I became much closer and I was commanded with more firmness and authority. One of my principal jobs was to calm down the unruly group and bring order to the assembly. I will say that there were times when I took some pretty heavy knocks. At other times, it was almost a breeze, with just a light tap here and there. I do have a few dents and bumps on my head to show for the real tough battles. On a couple of occasions, my boss and I had to ask for assistance from armed police officers, as well as undercover agents. Threats had been made. It turned out, however, that they were idle threats.

The normal hitch of service was two years. However, my boss signed me up for four hitches, eight years. I was getting a little weary toward the end of our campaigns. For example, our copper smelter went down after much encouragement for closure from environmentalists, including Governor Bruce Babbit.

Also, the area's principal employer, Phelps Dodge Corporation, moved its general offices from our city to Phoenix, causing a devastating loss of highly paid jobs. To compound these problems, the Mexican peso devalued against the dollar, and our merchants suffered accordingly.

On one occasion, the governor of Sonora contacted my boss in the wintertime, when the highway from Agua Prieta to Janos, Chihuahua, was closed because of snow in the mountains. He requested assistance to clear the road so that traffic could pass. My boss arranged through the Arizona governor's office for this to be accomplished.

In 1987, my CO took me to Phoenix when he was elected president of the Arizona League of Cities and Towns, a group comprised of some eighty-seven Arizona municipalities. This was really light duty compared to duty on the home front.

In the early summer of 1988, I knew that my tour of duty was about to end. I was looking forward to a rest. The actual retirement date and appropriate retirement ceremonies occurred on June 8, 1988. At that time, my boss laid me on the shelf, and since then I have been peacefully retired.

All I ask is that during my retirement you occasionally dust me, admire the patina I developed over my years of use, and recall with appreciation the assistance I gave during my active service. All you need say is "Gavel, rest in peace!"

BORDER TURMOIL

During the first week of April 2005, there was a great clamor and a lot of attention directed to the U.S.-Mexico border illegal alien situation. The militaristic Minutemen were assembling at Tombstone and Douglas, Arizona, to "assist" the U.S. Border Patrol in capturing undocumented Mexicans in the United States.

All the television and radio stations were full of the "news," and on the first day of the gathering of the Minutemen in Tombstone, it was reported that there were more newsmen present than Minutemen.

This brought to mind a time in July of 1985, when I was mayor of Douglas and there was political strife on the Mexican side of the border. Agua Prieta was having an election for mayor. Leonardo Yañez had been *presidente municipál* (same as mayor) of Agua Prieta for approximately three years. He was the first member of the PAN party (*Partido Acción National*) (the conservative National Action Party) to be elected *presidente municipál* since the founding of the PRI party (*Partido Nacional Revolucionario*) (National Revolutionary Party) in Agua Prieta in 1929.

I was concerned because of all the unrest in our closest neighboring city. The turmoil was the result of the intense animosity and hatred of the liberal revolutionary faction on the one hand, and the conservative government and Catholic-oriented group on the other.

I met with my police chief, Alvaro Fragoso, who was professionally trained to deal with civil disorder. A number of ugly incidents had been reported in Agua Prieta, caused by the intensity of the political race. The PRI party was desperately committed to regaining control in the city of its birth. There were reports of beatings and *halcones* (toughs) walking the streets with clubs, inflicting injuries on innocent bystanders.

A great number of wealthy Mexicans and PAN sympathizers had decided it was a good time to "take a vacation" in the United States. Many had crossed with their families, going to such places as Douglas, Tucson, San Diego, and La Jolla. They planned to stay until the situation returned to normal.

I called Al Fragoso to talk about the problem in the event a great number of Mexicans "bolted" the border to escape into the United States, most especially into Douglas. We had worked out plans with the Cochise County sheriff's department, the United States Border Patrol, and other police agencies to handle such a contingency. We had even arranged to make plans to feed and house refugees at the Cochise County fairgrounds if it became necessary.

About this time, I received a telephone call from the Arizona governor's office in Phoenix and was told that two television employees from channel 12, one a reporter and the other a cameraman, had crossed the border near Agua Prieta the previous day and had not been seen or heard from since that time. Their families were frantic and the governor's office was concerned as well. I was asked if I could assist in finding out anything about these two and aid in their safe return.

I called Al and briefed him on the situation. He said he had two Hispanic officers who were well connected with the police in Agua Prieta. He would send them over the border, out of uniform, to inquire about the television personnel.

A few hours had elapsed when Al called me and said, "Mayor, my officers have returned and they tell me that there is no government in place in Agua Prieta." This meant no city police, officials, or staff. "The city hall has been burned and several city police cars have been burned as well," he reported. He went on to say, "We were unable to find out anything about the two TV crewmen. We do feel that once identified as Americans and television reporters, however, they will be permitted to return to the United States without any problems."

I informed the governor's office of these events and told them that we expected the TV people to pop through the border fence at some point.

Later that day, I received a call from the governor's office telling me that the two TV people had crossed the border with all their equipment intact and that they were safe and sound. They had been busy gathering stories and were waiting until things calmed down before returning to the United States.

The government in Agua Prieta returned to normal after several weeks with the election of a new PRI mayor. No new problems were reported.

MEXICAN TIME

In 1986, Sieman's company dedicated the opening of its new *maquiladora* (assembly) plant in Agua Prieta, the city across the border from Douglas. Sieman's is a large German engineering company which makes electronic products.

The Agua Prieta plant assembled restraining devices such as seat belts for cars and airplanes. It was a large plant which planned to employ a lot of people who desperately needed work. One of my clients had built the building for Sieman's—a fine facility, completely new and state-of-the-art. Because I was mayor of Douglas at the time, I was an invited guest at the opening. Governor Rodolfo Felix-Valdez of Sonora was speaker of the day. He had flown in to Agua Prieta's small dirt airport for the occasion. The mayor of Agua Prieta, Leonardo Yañez, and leaders of both business communities were in attendance.

It was a grand and glorious occasion. A tour of the plant was set for 11:30 in the morning, followed by a sumptuous luncheon scheduled for 12:00 noon. I had attended a great number of similar functions in Mexico and was accustomed to the fact that they invariably started about an hour late. But not on this day.

When I arrived at 12:30 and entered the large reception hall, I found the group seated, the governor in the place of honor, and the seat to his right (reserved for me) already taken. There was no room for me at the head table, nor at any other table for that matter. I stood and watched while the group ate and visited. I saw the governor speak to one of his aides, who approached and told me that Governor

Felix wanted to meet with me in a small conference room after lunch.

When lunch ended, I met with the governor and his staff. Also present were Mayor Yañez and his staff. In an attempt to inject a little levity into a very awkward situation, I said in my best Spanish, "Governor, I am very sorry to be late for this occasion, but I expected you would be running on Mexican time."

He quickly responded in perfect English, "Mayor Williams, I consider it rude to be late for appointments and I pride myself on always being prompt."

Stunned, all I could say was, "You are the only Mexican government official I have ever met who adheres to that idea, and I compliment you, sir."

(So much for "Mexican time.")

MY SPEECH

The invitation was signed by Warden Fred Flannigan and read,

Dear Mayor: You are invited to the dedication of Papago Unit, Douglas Prison, on August 15, 1987. You will be asked to say a few words.

I dressed for the occasion in suit and tie. A beastly hot day. The ceremony was held outside–no shade. Long-winded speeches from the governor's representative, a member of the Cochise County Board of Supervisors, and Warden Flannigan.

After a long time, I was introduced with, "Now we will have a couple of words from Mayor Williams."

I took the microphone and said, "Thank you."

And returned to my seat hearing a loud round of applause.

Author, Mayor of Douglas 1980-1988

HONORARY GRAND MARSHALS

On July 3, 2005, my family (all twelve of us) motored to Douglas, where I rode in the annual Fourth of July parade. This was a special Fourth of July since it commemorated the 100-year anniversary of the founding of the city.

As mayor (from 1980 to 1988), I had been asked to ride in the parade as a grand marshal along with two other former mayors (Al Rodrigues and Liz Ames), also honored grand marshals.

The night before the parade and after dinner, my son-in-law Todd and my daughter Katie, along with their children, Natalie, age eight, and Pierce, age four, went along and spent the night with Daisy and me in a delightful bed-and-breakfast. The Hummingbird Bed and Breakfast was established in the very luxurious home of a former friend who lived in Douglas. It is now owned by Dorothy Millet. Dorothy is very spry and vigorous in spite of her advanced age. One of the delights of staying at the Hummingbird is that she is a gourmet cook and her breakfasts rank with the best any four-star hotel has to offer.

On July 3, we ate dinner at the Howling Coyote Restaurant, located in the boonies fifteen miles west of Douglas. The Howling Coyote specialized in steaks and beans, and the fare was delicious.

After a good night's rest, we feasted on a breakfast of fresh fruit compote, small pancakes (both plain and blueberry), homemade coffeecake, crisp bacon and scrambled eggs, orange juice and coffee. What a wonderful way to start the day!

Then: Dad as mayor of Douglas riding Spot in 1948 Rodeo parade,
flanked by Ruby Eicks, rodeo queen, on his right.

The rest of the family from Phoenix had come down to Douglas after spending the night in Tucson, having left early so as to arrive in time for the 10:00 a.m. start of the parade.

I had made arrangements with Robyn Brekhus for the family to view the parade from the Gadsden Hotel balcony. This was where the local radio station had its setup and was an excellent location for watching.

Natalie and Pierce rode with me in a sleek white convertible driven by Julie Johnson Romero.

Pierce was apprehensive about sitting on the deck above the rear seat. "Grampsy, don't let me fall!" was his cry.

Now: Author and grandchildren, Natalie and Pierce, grand marshals in Fourth of July parade
celebrating the 100-year anniversary of the founding of Douglas

"I'll hang on to you, Pierce, don't worry," I assured him.

We assembled at Third Street and G Avenue, the parade's starting point. It was sometime after 10:00 o'clock–late, as is customary for such Douglas events. After the late start, we heard the loud reports of fireworks signifying the start of the parade, and we were underway.

It was a very hot day and a slow-moving parade–needless to say, uncomfortable except for the fact that we were enjoying ourselves immensely. Nat, Pierce, and I waved to the assembled crowd as we rode along G Avenue.

As our car neared the Gadsden, we waved with enthusiastic vigor to the family, hoping they would get some good pictures of us.

After the parade, the whole family went to the Douglas-Williams House museum, which had been my home in my high school years. Before this special Fourth of July, I had made arrangements with Nan Ames, a stalwart official of the Douglas Historical Society, to show us the museum, which proved to be a wonderful experience for us.

Dad had bought the house when I was a high school freshman, and I lived in it until I went away to military school as a high school junior. After New Mexico Military Institute, I attended the University of Arizona, subsequently married, and went into the army.

After Dad's death in 1983, I made arrangements with the State of Arizona to acquire the home, with the understanding that it would be converted from a residence into a museum. This was accomplished with the assistance of some of my friends in the State Historical Society and the state legislature. I did the law work to form an Arizona nonprofit corporation, the Douglas Historical Society. The Arizona State Historical Society and the Douglas Society entered into an agreement whereby the Douglas group provided docents and general care for the home, while the state provided the capital expenditures necessary to keep the property in good condition.

In the afternoon, after lunch at the Gadsden, we drove back to Tucson and spent the evening celebrating Pierce's fourth birthday, though his actual birth date falls on the seventh.

Everyone had a fine time, and many fond memories from that day are placed in the family's collective memory. In particular, I shall always remember riding with *my two honorary grand marshals*, Natalie and Pierce.